NICOLA MORGAN

KNOW YOUR BRAIN

Feed it ★ Test it ★ Stretch it

D1385393

WALKER BOOKS
AND SUBSIDIARIES

LONDON · BOSTON · SYDNEY · AUCKLAND

CONTENTS

✏️ THE KNOW YOUR BRAIN QUIZ

First, you need to take this quiz. Why?
You'll find out later...

Get a piece of paper. Write your name and today's date on it.

Then write the title of this quiz: **Know Your Brain.**

Read each statement from **A–J** and choose one of these numbers for each one:

1 = agree a lot
2 = agree a bit
3 = don't agree or disagree
4 = disagree a bit
5 = disagree a lot

Then, on your piece of paper, record your answers. So, for example, if you disagreed a bit with statement **A,** write **A4**.

A I know a lot about how the brain works.

1   2   3   4   5

B I have a good brain and I think I am clever.

1   2   3   4   5

C Most people of my age are cleverer than I am.

1   2   3   4   5

D I believe that I will be successful in life.

1 2 3 4 5

E Some people are good at everything.

1 2 3 4 5

F I know exactly what my skills and weaknesses are.

1 2 3 4 5

G I can't change the way my brain is.

1 2 3 4 5

H People who are the cleverest at school
will be most successful later too.

1 2 3 4 5

I Clever people always do well in tests at school.

1 2 3 4 5

J Everyone would learn better if they sat at a
tidy desk, with quiet music in the background.

1 2 3 4 5

When you've done them all, hide the piece of paper
somewhere safe and don't look at it again until I tell
you to. Don't forget where you put it!

HOW THIS BOOK WORKS

There is a lot for you to do in this book. The quizzes and exercises will help you find out different things about your brain. At the end of some chapters you can 'Test: Your New Knowledge'. You could get a new notebook to record your answers in – then they'll all be in one place and it will be an interesting record of your brain and who you are. You may want to read more about the research behind this book. When you see a little number by a word like this: experts[2] go to pages 200–204 and find the number 2; that will show you how to find more information. These are called 'endnotes'.

STOP!!!!! BRAIN BOOST

A brain boost is a treat for your brain, something that helps it work well. Your brain is like any machine – it sometimes needs more fuel, a rest, fresh air, a new activity, or a bit of attention.

Every time you see the words **BRAIN BOOST**, choose any of the choices on pages 187–192.

You can also do a brain boost at any time you need to.

When your brain is refreshed, you may go on. It's very important that you WANT to. And that you are feeling happy. Scientists know that we learn better when we are feeling happy and when we WANT to do the task.

BRAIN CHECK:

At the beginning of each chapter, you'll see this sign **BRAIN** ☀☺ **CHECK** – you should do this brain check before starting the chapter. You can record your answers in your notebook or on a piece of paper.

Read each statement.

If you think 'Not at all', put a ☀☺ beside it.
If you think, 'Well, a bit, maybe', put a ?.
If you think, 'Yes, definitely', put a ✔.

I am tired.
I am thirsty.
I am hungry.
I am in a bad mood.
I am physically uncomfortable.
It's too noisy for me.
Something is distracting me.
I wish I was doing something else.

You need EIGHT ☀☺.
If you have any ✔ or ?, can you do something to change them into ☀☺?
I suppose you can have one ?, but only if you feel that it is really not bothering you.

Chapter 1

WHY READ THIS BRAINY BOOK?

Because your brain is special ~ Because your brain is
YOU ~ Because your brain needs you ~ Because you
will discover your intelligence, and be surprised...
~ Hang on! How do we know about brains?

Because your brain is special

Nothing is more amazing than the human brain. Billions and billions (and a whole load more billions) of cells work together in ways that we don't fully understand yet. Maybe we never will.

And every single brain is different. Even if you have an identical twin, your twin's brain is not identical to yours, because our brains are also affected by things that happen to us and those things will be slightly different for each twin. You'll meet different people; those people will say different things to you; you'll sometimes make a different choice. And those differences will make you each different. The older you get, the more different you'll be because more different things will have happened to you – and therefore to your brain.

Even having a different thought changes your brain. Your brain is also cleverer than the cleverest

11

computer. Computers can store huge numbers of facts, work out enormous sums and sort through vast amounts of information; but computers can only do what humans program them to do and they work in a very different way from brains. Things like seeing, thinking, feeling, imagining, wondering, understanding body language, and many types of decisions, are things that only brains can do. And remember – it was humans who made computers, and not the other way round!

One of the things humans can do much better than computers is to see. Of course, cameras can record perfectly what's in front of them but no one has yet invented anything that can see like a human. Because it's not just about recording what's in front of us: it's also about knowing what it is. To a computer, it's just a meaningless mixture of lines and shadows.

For example, imagine you see a picture of a dog. You *know* it's a dog. But it isn't exactly the same as any of the other dogs you've seen, so how do you know it's a dog? After all, a Great Dane is nothing like a Jack Russell and yet somehow you know they're both dogs. 'Well, it's got four legs and a tail.' Yes, but so has a cat. 'OK, so it wags its tail.' No, this is a **STILL** picture. And even if you only saw its head you'd know it was a dog. Even if it was a breed of dog you'd never seen, your amazing human brain would know it's a dog and not a cat. No computer can do that.

Every time we look at something, our brains are

doing incredibly complicated things to make sense of it, by measuring, adapting, interpreting, understanding, remembering, comparing, categorizing, assessing, and making all sorts of instant decisions that you hardly have time to think about. Computers are way behind. Even my dog can see better than a computer – and you will learn quite a lot about how unclever my dog is...

Understanding what we hear is complicated too. You can tell what I'm feeling just from the way I say some words. Imagine me saying this sentence: 'I really believe you.' Depending on how I say it, I could mean I **DO** believe you; or I could mean I completely **DON'T** believe you. But when you hear me, you will know *EXACTLY* which I mean. A computer just can't do that.

There's no getting away from it – brains are amazing.

Because your brain is YOU

Inside your brain is everything that makes you you. You may think your legs and arms and eyes and ears are important, but you'd still be *you* without them. You could lose a leg and you'd still be you; you could have a heart transplant or a false hand, but you'd still be you. You'd still wake up in the morning and know who you are.

But imagine you had a brain transplant. (It's not possible but imagine it anyway.) You simply wouldn't be you any more. In **YOUR** brain are all *your* memories, your skills, your fears, your hopes, your tastes, everything you know, the reasons why you do everything. Your brain allows you to do anything from breathing to kicking a ball, everything from sneezing to laughing, from maths or music to drama or reading. Your brain allows you to *decide* to do some things – like sitting down or standing up; and it *makes* you do some things you might not choose to do, like crying, or laughing, or coughing, or sleeping. Your brain makes you happy, sad, angry, afraid, tired, confused, shocked, hungry.

So, does your brain control you? In some ways. But in some ways not. **YOU** can control your brain as well. Because **YOU** can control some of the things that happen to it and you can make some choices.

Because your brain needs you

There are things you can choose to do that will make your brain more brilliant than it already is – and there are some things you can do that will damage it. You need to know what's good for your brain and what's bad for it – because when your brain is damaged, it doesn't repair easily. Sometimes, it doesn't repair at all.

And one thing is certain – you can't have another brain. You are stuck with the one you've got, so make the most of it.

It IS brilliant – and by the time you've read this book it will be more brilliant. This book shows you how to care for your brain and make it as wonderful as possible, simply by choosing to know it and care for it.

Because you will discover your intelligence, and be surprised...

What about geniuses? Brilliant successes? Do you think they're the people who did well at school? The school successes? Well, think again. Many of the world's greatest successes and even geniuses did badly at school; they didn't fit in, or shine; they sometimes failed exams; often their teachers despaired! Some of them had dyslexia, epilepsy, depression, difficult childhoods, language and learning difficulties, lots of reasons why people did not think they'd be so successful later on.

How come? Because 'intelligence' is **MUCH** more complicated than anything that is tested at school. There are many types of intelligence. So lots of people feel stupid at school, but are extremely successful later. If you are finding life difficult at school, if you seem to think differently from other people and just can't seem to do what is expected of you, perhaps you have an excuse – perhaps you should say, 'Well, it's just the genius in me!' You might like to know that Dr Seuss, the famous children's author, was voted 'student least likely to succeed' – but he has sold around half a billion – that's half a **BILLION** – copies of his books. Some failure!

In Chapter 5, you will see that there are many ways

of being intelligent, some of which you may not have thought of. You may discover that you are brilliant in a way that you didn't know counted. You could even be a genius...

This book tells you how the brain works – although we don't know everything yet. Then it shows you how **YOUR** brain works – because people's brains don't all work in exactly the same way – and how to make it work in the best way it can. There are quizzes to find your strengths and weaknesses, and ways to use that knowledge to make schoolwork easier. I will show you ways in which you **CAN** control your brain – and make it better and bigger. And the ways of improving your brain are nearly all fun. Some of them even involve eating, or laughing and playing games. It's not all about hard work. In fact, it's about making life easier.

Your brain is going to be with you for the rest of your life. It will grow and change with you. It **IS** you – it contains your history, and a large part of your future too. Know and train your brain and you will affect your life in more ways than you can imagine.

Hang on! How do we know about brains?

Until about ten years ago, everything we knew about brains came from either cutting up dead ones or from special X-rays and scans. But there are problems with that: if you have to wait for someone to die before you can look inside their brain, you won't find out how it works, because then it's ... er ... not working. And the special X-rays and scans were a bit risky, so you could only do them to ill people who really needed an investigation – and you still wouldn't know what normal, healthy brains do.

So, when a new and very safe machine came along in the 1990s, this made a huge difference. It was called ... take a deep breath .... functional Magnetic Resonance Imaging. Let's call it fMRI, because that's what the experts call it. (And when they write it they always put a small f and capital MRI. Why? To be awkward? To be mysterious? Because they feel like it? Because someone didn't teach them about capital letters? I don't know. If your brain wants to know, go and find out.)

fMRI does two things: it gives us a detailed picture of inside someone's brain but it also – and this is the really clever part – *tells us which parts of the brain are working* when the person does something.

For example, if you are in the scanner and the scientist says, 'Think of something funny,' or 'Think of something you hate,' or 'Count backwards from twenty,' or 'Imagine a cold wet slimy worm is crawling down your neck...' the parts of your brain that you are using light up. So, scientists can see what normal brains do – and they can see if someone's brain is working differently.

I can't show you pictures of the inside of your brain. But I can show you a lot about how brains work, how **YOUR** brain works, and how to make it work as well as it possibly can. Get ready to know it and grow it!

People sometimes ask me why I am so interested in brains. How could anyone *NOT* be? That's my only answer. The human brain is the most amazing thing in the world. And you have one, right inside your head. Let's take a look...

Chapter 2

BRAIN BASICS

What a brain is like ~ Our big brains ~ How it works~
A word about babies ~ Your brain at different ages

What a brain is like

Your brain is about the size of a very large grapefruit. It weighs around 1.5 kg – roughly the same as an adult's. That's about the weight of twelve apples.

It is soft and wet and horribly mushy! It is also very fragile but is well protected by your tough skull. It's a disgusting grey colour with veins across the surface – not very tasty-looking (although some people used to believe that eating brains made you clever).

It's wrinkly too, and shaped like a walnut. In fact, the human brain is much more wrinkly than most other animal brains – certainly wrinklier than the brains of cats and dogs. Why? Because, in human brains, the outer covering, or **cortex**, is extremely large and packed full of brain cells; so when it's squashed and wrapped round the smaller inner parts, it becomes very creased.

To picture this, think of two pieces of paper – a small one and a large one. If you had to squash each one to fit inside a small box, you'd find the larger one would have more creases. Try it if you aren't sure.

All mammals have a cortex; reptiles and birds have a much simpler one; fish have an almost non-existent one, and insects have none. The cortex is necessary for all the difficult thinking that we do. Not much thinking goes on in a beetle's brain, believe me.

> **BRAINY FACT** The human cortex is only about two millimetres thick – much thinner than it looks in pictures. But if you unfolded its wrinkles and spread it out it would cover about the same area as a pillowcase.

Actually, humans don't have the wrinkliest brains. Some whales' brains are wrinklier, for example. So, although wrinkliness is important, brains are not simple things and don't follow simple rules. Human brains seem to be so clever *PARTLY* because of wrinkliness, **PARTLY** because of size, and ***PARTLY*** because of very special ways in which the sections work together. So, wrinkly may be good, but it's definitely not everything.

Our big brains

Our brains are very big compared with other animals' brains, especially when related to the size of our bodies. Most other animals have smaller brains, and much less cortex. The parts of the cortex at the front of our heads – the **frontal** and **prefrontal cortex** – are especially well developed in humans. That's where the cleverest thinking happens – including most of the things that make us different from other animals.

Scientists used to think that humans have a bigger frontal cortex than *ALL* other animals, even apes, but this now seems not to be true. It does depend how you measure it – and that's not easy because our bodies are different sizes. It's fair to say that there may be very little difference between the size of the frontal cortex in humans and some apes, for example – not enough to explain how humans can do so much more than apes which may have a similar or larger frontal cortex.

It may also be that it's just one or two **PARTS** of the frontal cortex that are most important, and maybe those are much bigger in humans. We don't know yet. Wrinkliness and size seem to be parts of the answer, but are definitely not the whole answer. The special ways in which the parts of the human brain work together are things we don't yet understand perfectly.

BRAINY FACT Hummingbirds and fruit-eating squirrel monkeys both have a bigger brain than humans when compared with body size. The human brain is about 2% of our total weight; the hummingbird's[1] is about 3.8% and the squirrel monkey's somewhere between 3.2 and 5% – experts[2] can't agree. Maybe the experts aren't brainy enough. A hummingbird would probably know.

How it works

The wrinkly, mushy grey stuff in your brain is made of different sorts of cells. The most important ones are called **neurons**. You have about 100 billion of them. That's 100,000,000,000. About sixteen times as many as the number of people on Earth.

Here's how to imagine a neuron. Think of a tree – it has a trunk, a chunky bit at the top of the trunk and lots of branches coming off the chunky bit.

The trunk is called the **axon**.

The chunky bit is the main body of the neuron.

The branches are called **dendrites**.

Now, stop thinking about a tree because...

A A neuron is **TINY**. Definitely not big enough for a bird's nest. More the size of a grain of sand, with a baby daddy-long-legs leg coming off it. If you have normal eyesight, you can just about see a neuron – if you look closely.

B A neuron does the opposite of a tree: a tree draws its food UP from the ground through its trunk and into the branches but a neuron sends its messages **DOWN** the trunk (axon) and into the branches (dendrites) of other neurons.

BRAINY FACT Your brain contains **10,000 miles of fibres connecting all your neurons to each other.**

The axons and dendrites carry the messages

A Neuron

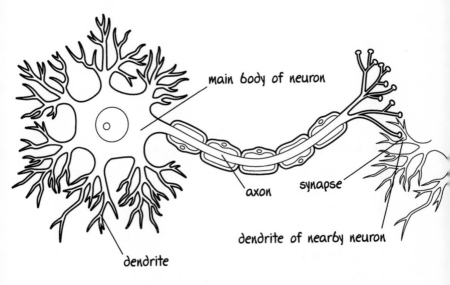

main body of neuron

axon

synapse

dendrite of nearby neuron

dendrite

between neurons. The place where an axon meets a dendrite is called a **synapse**. Actually, they don't meet, not quite – there's a *TINY* gap. How tiny? Definitely so small you couldn't see it. If you can imagine this (because I can't) it's a 200,000th of a millimetre. That's a millimetre cut into 200,000 pieces. The message jumps across the synapse. Messages are flying around your brain incredibly fast – the fastest can be going at 120 metres a second.

Some neurons have as many as 100,000 dendrites, so they might be connected to 100,000 other neurons. And each one of those could send messages to the same number of other cells. Etc. Etc.

Etc. Etc. And very many of them will be working at the same time, sending different messages for a whole load of thoughts and actions. The number of different paths the messages could take is impossible to imagine – so many billions and trillions that you'll go dizzy thinking about it and it would take an expert mathematician to work out how many zeros to write.

BRAINY FACT Neurons may be incredibly important, but they're not the only sort of brain cell. And they're not the most numerous. Your brain has even more glial cells and scientists are beginning to understand exactly what they do. They help take food to the brain and clean up dead cells. They are the brain's waiters and cleaners. When scientists find out more, maybe we'll discover they are secretaries and janitors as well. They might even be the secret police and the government all rolled into one. But the neurons are the workers, and very clever and hardworking they are too.

Neurons sending messages

Messages are electrical currents. So, your brain is fizzing with electricity and everything you do needs these little electrical messages. Without them, you'd never be able to move a finger, jump a wall, breathe, sneeze, go to the toilet, or have any thoughts. The neurons produce the electricity and also pass it along to other neurons.

If you want to move your hand, the part of your brain where you decide to move your hand sends an electrical message to the part that controls the muscles and nerves in your hand, and your hand moves. You aren't aware of thinking about it, because it happens so fast.

A word about babies

A baby is born with around 100 billion neurons as well, but not many dendrites on them, and therefore not many connections. That's why a baby can't do much – though it can do quite a lot of things, such as breathing, eating and crying. It's very good at crying.

So how does a baby learn?

The same way as you and I learn – by trying. Every time we try to do something, even if we don't succeed at first, we start to grow dendrites and then connections between cells. As we get better at something, we grow more dendrites and connections – and then those dendrites become stronger, until we are very good at it.

If you watch a tiny baby, you'll notice that it doesn't seem to focus very well. It looks in the right direction but it doesn't seem to know what it's seeing. That's because it has to learn to see – it has to learn WHAT the things are that it sees, how far away they are, whether they are frightening, what they mean, which ones are important. (These are some things a computer can't do.) At first, everything is jumbled and meaningless for the baby, but gradually it learns how to see and understand what it sees; it grows new connections between the neurons in its brain. Simply by trying.

BRAINY FACT Scientists have recently discovered things they call **mirror neurons.** These become active when we watch someone else do something, and then the same neurons send signals when we plan to do the thing ourselves. So, if a baby watches someone smile, certain neurons fire in a certain pattern; then, when the baby tries to smile, those neurons are already set up, so that the baby has a better chance of being able to do it. And not just babies – we all do it. When we watch someone do something, our mirror neurons fire up – and when we actually try to do the same thing, our neurons will be ready to fire in the same pattern.

Your brain at different ages
Baby in the womb

- Five months *BEFORE* birth, a baby has about 200 billion neurons – but this is far more than we need, so about half of them die before birth.
- In some parts – such as the parts responsible for breathing – the neurons have lots of dendrites and synapses, so they work well. But other parts – such as the parts responsible for language – have

few connections between neurons. This picture here shows how the neurons in a baby's brain might look at different ages.

A baby's brain at birth   ... and at 15 months

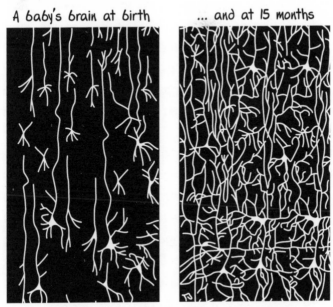

showing how lots of dendrites have grown.

Birth—10

✱ A newborn baby has about 100 billion neurons – similar to an adult (**BUT** some will die and others will grow before the baby reaches adulthood). Dendrites and connections grow very fast in the first few years. The time of fastest dendrite growth is at around eight months. The more different things a child experiences, the easier it will be to learn – as dendrites and connections will grow strongly in all areas of the brain.

- New neurons also grow, usually in spurts – for example, lots of new neurons grow at around age two.

- During the first three years of life, a child learns to understand much of what he or she sees and hears; develops the basics of language and communication; is able to walk, run, balance, hit and throw; learns to manipulate things with his or her hands and even to form some letters and pictures.

- By around twenty-four months, a baby knows that the figure in the mirror is HIM or HER and not another child! By about four years, a child begins to realize what is in his or her mind may be different from what is in someone else's mind – something which psychologists[3] believe other animals cannot do, though some apes, such as chimpanzees, seem to be able to in a very simple way.

- Scientists believe that some things must be learned by a certain age or the child will not be able to learn them properly. These ages are called 'windows', and we don't know why there are windows for some skills and not others. For example:

  • a child who cannot see (perhaps because of a condition called cataracts) before the age of about two, will **NEVER** see properly, even if the cataracts are later cured;

  • a child who doesn't hear any words or experience

language at all before the age of twelve won't learn speech;

    • a child who does not start a foreign language before the age of seven may learn to speak the language fluently but won't have a perfect accent.

❂ With many other things – such as playing a musical instrument, painting, playing football – there's no special age you must start them by. (Though it's generally *EASIER* earlier.)

❂ A human brain has something called **PLASTICITY**, which means it is changed by what happens to it; and a child's brain is more 'plastic' than an adult's, because development has not finished. This is why it is easier to learn many things before you are an adult.

10-11 for girls and 11-12 for boys[4] (but these are averages so you might be earlier or later)

❂ The teenage brain begins to develop, with huge numbers of new neurons growing. About 15–20 per cent extra neurons appear.

❂ Your brain begins to produce large amounts of the **hormones** that will eventually turn you into an adult man or woman – and that may also affect your feelings

❂ Your brain changes its sleep patterns – you may find it hard to go to sleep as early as you used to. And you may find it hard to get up in the morning. Blame your brain!

12–15[5]

- The middle stage for the teenage brain – many neurons die: around 15–20 per cent seems normal. During this time, the brain keeps the neurons it finds useful. The important thing here is the brain's special rule: **USE IT OR LOSE IT**. What you don't use, you lose. So *USE* lots of parts of your brain!

- During this time, parts of the brain may not communicate well with each other and some skills may be lost for a while – for example, at this age you may be less good at recognizing what someone else is feeling or thinking.

- Other changes in your brain may mean that you judge risks less well and you may do things that you wouldn't have done before. You may make bad decisions.

16–23[6]

- Full adult development happens during this time. All the connections that are left after the 12–15 stage become stronger. This means you can be very good at the things you are good at but it's a little harder to learn new things. (But you *can* learn new things at any age – there's no excuse for your mum, dad, teachers, grandparents...)

- The wrinkly outer layer, the cortex, becomes 20 per cent thicker during the teenage years, because of extra dendrites and thickened axons.

23+

From this time, you are more likely to lose cells than grow them. But, we have *far* more neurons than we need, so losing cells does not mean becoming less clever.

What usually happens with adults is this...

1 We do the things we are good at and avoid the things we feel bad at, because we're lazy and complete wimps. And you thought adults could do everything? No way: we just stick to what we're good at. And we **SHOULDN'T**. So, I stick to writing, talking and anything else to do with words, and avoid tennis, chess, music, dancing, aerobics, knitting, flower-arranging, role-playing, fast computer games, and anything to do with numbers.

2 So we become better at the things we are already good at – and worse at the things we are bad at.

3 And so the parts of our brain which were already weaker become even weaker.

4 Then, when someone asks us to do one of those difficult things, we can't, because we haven't practised, so we feel even worse about it. And we panic and avoid it completely. Which is wimpish and bad and, as you know by now, I do it all the time.

What we *SHOULD* do is activities to help all the parts of our brain, not just the strong ones.

Actually, I am not quite as bad as I make out. I am

working on my memory, logic and number skills, for example. But not tennis. I also tried to learn a musical instrument – I was terrible at it, but at least I tried. If only I'd tried it when I was your age... Just think of all those neurons, ready and waiting, now gone forever.

But when I was your age, this information about brain development was not known. Scientists thought that no new brain cells could grow after the age of between three and five and that after about the age of six no physical development took place in the brain. You already know more about brains than I did at your age: make the most of it and become cleverer than your parents – and me!

Time for a **BRAIN** 💡 **BOOST** – choose an oxygen boost and a fuel boost from p 187 and p190.

 **Test: Your New Knowledge**

Let's see what you have learned in this chapter. First, though, a few tips for easy learning.

- ✪ **Read things twice.** When you read it a second time, it's more likely to stay in your head – it helps put it into a different part of your memory, where it might stay.
- ✪ It also helps if you **write something** as well as SEEING it.
- ✪ And if you **read it aloud.**
- ✪ SOME people find it easier to learn things when they are lying on the floor; SOME people like to listen to music while they learn. **Do whichever feels comfortable for YOU.**

If you have a special notebook, use that. Or get a piece of paper.

You do not have to do the test from memory. Find the answers in Chapters 1 and 2. **SPEAK** the answers as you **WRITE** them. If you want to draw a picture, do. Display the answers in any way you like. After all, I can't see you. I'm not that clever.

Then, if you want to, decorate your answers – colour them, draw cartoons, give them faces, anything at all, but something that you enjoy. That way, you will remember them better.

1 What's the special scanning method that lets scientists see what the brain is doing?
2 How much does your brain weigh?
3 Your brain is ____ per cent of your body weight.
4 Which part of the brain becomes 15–20 per cent thicker during teenage years?
5 Approximately how many neurons does a normal brain have?
6 Messages go along the _____ into the _____ of another _____ .
7 What's the word for the connection (or tiny space) between neurons?
8 Is the human brain more wrinkly or less wrinkly than a cat's?
9 What's the brain's rule that makes it decide which neurons to keep?
10 Who normally develops towards being a teenager first – girls or boys?

What can you remember?

When you have found the answers, and done your best to learn them, give the notebook/paper to someone else and ask them to test you.

It's not so important what you scored – though you did brilliantly if you scored 8/10 or more. More important is whether you can remember it tomorrow. And next week. To help you do this, read through the questions and answers again later. Then you can stun your teachers with facts about the brain.

Chapter 3
BRAINY PARTS

Brainy bits and what they do ~ Why can't we be good at everything? ~ Left brain/right brain ~ Are humans cleverer than other animals? ~ So, what's special about the human brain?

Brainy bits and what they do

Your brain has lots of different parts. The parts have different jobs. But most actions need several parts of your brain working well together.

Imagine playing the guitar. You have to do all these different things at once:

- move your fingers fast and accurately – with both hands doing completely different things;
- deal with rhythm and timing;
- remember the notes;
- follow the music with your eyes;
- remember things your teacher said;
- feel and express the emotion or style of the piece;
- perhaps also move your foot and body in rhythm.

That's a lot of different activities, and many brain parts will all be working together.

The Brain from Above

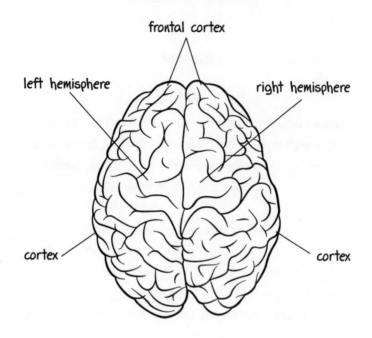

frontal cortex

left hemisphere

right hemisphere

cortex

cortex

Outside the brain

Here's what the brain looks like from the outside. You are looking at it from above. You'll see two halves – the left **hemisphere** and the right hemisphere, covered by the cortex. They are similar but not exactly the same. They are joined by a thick cable called the **corpus callosum**. The two halves communicate with each other through this cable and although they work in slightly different ways they do work together.

Almost every part has a matching partner in the

other hemisphere. For example, both halves contain a **hippocampus**, a **thalamus**, and a **hypothalamus**. But there is only one **pineal gland**, right in the middle; and two small areas, called **Broca's** and **Wernicke's** areas, are only present on the left.

Hidden beneath the brain, at the back of your head, is the **brainstem**. This controls things like breathing and your heart beat.

Tucked underneath the main brain, near the brainstem, is the **cerebellum**, which means 'little brain' – because it looks like a small version of the brain. The cerebellum also has two halves. It has a huge range of uses, especially to do with movement.

Inside the brain

The cortex is wrapped round a whole collection of parts called the **limbic system**. Reptiles and birds have a limbic system too.

The limbic system is where emotional reactions and instincts happen. This does not mean that reptiles such as lizards are sitting around feeling emotional and weeping all day – just that they don't do much thinking before scurrying away from something frightening. They just scurry. Scurrying is absolutely the best thing to do when your limbic system tells you there's a large foot about to stamp on you. You don't want to hang around being philosophical or working out the speed and angle at which the foot is coming towards your ......erghhhhh. Scrunch.

The Limbic System

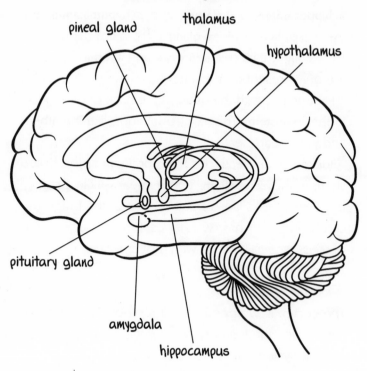

pineal gland

thalamus

hypothalamus

pituitary gland

amygdala

hippocampus

The limbic system has several parts:

Hippocampus – important for memory and learning. With the lizard, this would be along the lines of, 'Stone being lifted, light coming in – seems familiar. Ah! Yes, last time that happened, Larry was scrunched by a huge foot... Better move. Fast!' Going back to you and your guitar-playing, the hippocampus is important for remembering notes and sequences, and many things to do with learning. and remembering how to do something.

Amygdala – involved in sudden strong emotions, such as fear and anger. A baby has a very well developed **amygdala**. And the lizard's is pretty good too – his instant fear of the large foot is what pushes him to act. Your amygdala could be active when you are feeling the emotion in the music you are playing on your guitar – whether it's happy, angry or gloomy.

Thalamus – information from all your senses (apart from smell) arrives here. It will be active as you listen to the music you are playing.

Hypothalamus – controls things like your body temperature, levels of chemicals, sleepiness, hunger and thirst – lots of functions that happen without you thinking or deciding or controlling.

Why can't we be good at everything?

All our brains are slightly different and work in slightly different ways. This is partly because we inherit skills and personalities from our parents (and grandparents and great-grandparents...); partly because different things happen to us in the womb and when we are tiny babies, which mean that our brains end up not exactly the same; and partly because of the learning experiences we have in early childhood – and later.

Whatever the reasons, some parts of your brain will be better developed and better organized than some parts of my brain.

Think about this: if a boy is born into a family with musical parents and lots of music in the house, he will have a good chance of being good at music. He could inherit his parents' ability, **AND** his parents will probably teach him early music skills. But, what if his personality makes him rebel against his parents' wishes, or he has an older sister who is so incredibly brilliant that he doesn't bother trying? Then he might not end up brilliant at music.

ALSO, a child in that family may have *LESS* chance of being good at football, or writing, or cooking, or something else that the family doesn't do so much of. Families make different choices and different choices make different brains.

There's not enough time in the day for you to learn to be good at everything. And our brains are not designed to be. When one brain part is exceptionally well developed, it seems that another part is often poorly developed or works less well.

For example, scientists have looked at the brain of Albert Einstein, one of the world's greatest ever scientists. Although some results are not clear, it seems that one brain part was larger than normal.[7] It also seems that another part[8] was smaller and one part[9] was missing. Of course, **MAYBE** the fact that these two parts were smaller or missing *HELPED* Einstein become brilliant. However, we also know that he was late learning to speak, and poor at spelling, and some experts believe he had a mild form of autism called **Asperger's**. He may well have been a genius, but he was not good at everything. His brain did not work 'perfectly'.

Scientists have also looked at the brains of London taxi drivers.[10] While cabbies might be no cleverer than anyone else (though they might disagree) they have to pass an extremely difficult exam called the 'Knowledge', which involves knowing every street in central London. It takes years to learn and many fail. The researchers noticed that London cabbies have a larger area at the back of the hippocampus. But ... they seem to have a smaller than normal area at the front of the hippocampus. So, it could well be that in growing a part of their brain while learning all that information, they lost another skill. What is it that London cabbies are less good at? The scientists are still working on it...

Left brain / right brain

Scientists have known since the 1950s that each half of the brain works a bit differently.

How did they know? Because of some operations to treat patients with very severe epilepsy. In these operations the corpus callosum was cut, so that the two brain halves were then separate. Both halves of the brain still worked, the epilepsy was often greatly improved, and many of the patients then lived healthy lives. But here are just two of the fascinating things that researchers noticed.

Whatsit? Thingumajig?

When scientists put a blindfold on a patient who had had this operation, and then put a pencil in his left hand, the patient could not say the name of the thing he was holding.[11] This is because the right brain controls the left side of the body – so the patient could *feel* the pencil, and 'knew what it was' – but the left side of the brain is where words and names are usually stored, so the patient could not say the name. He knew what it was but couldn't remember the name.

In two minds?

Scientists found that each brain half works in different ways, and almost has a different personality. In one amazing experiment, researchers[12] asked a patient the same question to each side of the brain separately[13]. They asked, 'What do you want to be?' The right brain said he wanted to be a racing driver. The left side said he wanted to be a draughtsman – a technical designer. Talk about being in two minds!

But what does this mean for us?

Well, scientists now understand some important differences between what the two halves do. Although both halves communicate with each other constantly and work together on nearly everything, and although nearly all the brain parts appear on both sides, each side has some different jobs to do and behaves a bit differently.

Some people believe that the way each of us behaves and thinks depends on whether our left or right brain hemisphere is stronger – or 'dominant'. People who believe this talk about being left-brained or right-brained.

This is what they say: the left brain is where simple maths takes place, so if you are very good at maths and some of the other things that the left brain does, your left brain is dominant.

The trouble with this is that the brain, as usual, is more complicated than any simple explanation can manage. Nearly everything we do uses **BOTH** halves, though in different ways. And if we have not had our brain halves separated by surgery, the information passes between the two halves so quickly that no one can say whether one half was being dominant.

Here's another illustration of how the brain is not simple enough for an easy explanation. The left brain is supposed to be better at lying and the right brain is more truthful. So, if you're a liar, does that mean you are left-brained? No, because in most people most language activities happen on the left – so even if your right brain wanted to tell the truth it couldn't because it usually doesn't control the speaking! And the more you think about that, the more you have to realize that it's much more complicated than some people make out.

On the other hand, thinking about your strengths and weaknesses is interesting and useful, as long as we don't make strict rules out of it.

Why can't we do a test?

Although tests for right/left brain dominance are fun, and may make you think in interesting ways about your own learning styles, I decided it would be wrong to include one in this book. Here's why...

- ✖ I don't think a test clearly shows you which half is dominant – depending on the wording of the questions, you'll get very different answers.
- ✖ Some people's brains work the other way round – some have their language areas on the right side instead of the left side, so the result won't mean anything because you won't know if you are one of those people.
- ✖ I don't agree that the science is strong enough or the conclusions clear enough.

But, if you are desperate, there are lots of free tests on the internet. Just search on the words 'brain hemisphere dominance test' and you'll come up with loads. I did – and got loads of different results. On Tuesday I was right-brained, on Wednesday morning I was left-brained and by lunchtime I was a complete mixture.

Even though I'm not testing you, I **DO** think it's interesting and perhaps useful to know some of the ways that scientists believe each brainy half works differently. But remember that any activity involves many different thoughts going on at the same time.

The left brain usually:

- deals with word meanings and names;
- tends to have a good sense of time;
- remembers the correct order of things;
- likes to sort things into categories;
- does simple sums;
- is logical;
- deals with facts;
- is better at lying and may have false memories;
- wants to know why things happen and to work things out.

The right brain usually:

- gets more information from pictures than words;
- recognizes faces, things, places;
- seeks patterns in things, makes connections;
- sees the whole picture rather than tiny details;
- is more truthful;
- uses the imagination;
- understands body language, emotion, tone of voice;
- specializes in music and art; is creative.

Some people suggest doing exercises and activities to 'strengthen' your 'weaker' side. There's no harm in doing such exercises – in other words, doing the things you find hard. But current science does not support the idea that you will make your left or right side 'stronger' – or that you need to. Both halves work beautifully together already.

I believe we work in many different ways, depending on what we are doing. Sometimes you need to be logical, and at other times you need to be imaginative; sometimes it's important to be organized, at others more relaxed; sometimes time is important, at others it's not; sometimes, you need to be truthful, and sometimes... And when you need to be logical, organized and punctual, the tidy left brain marches into perfect action as its skills come into play; when you need to be more imaginative, poetic, musical, then the dreamy right brain gets up and dances – but in each case, it is not only the left or right that's working: it's both, together, in harmony.

Are humans cleverer than other animals?

If we measure cleverness by things like building aeroplanes, inventing computers, doing maths, designing cathedrals and writing stories, then we are certainly cleverer than all other animals. But what if we measured cleverness by how well you could spin a spider web, or whether you could fly without a map the whole way from Africa to the Arctic? Spiders and birds would win then. Each animal can do something that humans can't.

But non-human animals act mostly by instinct – they are programmed to behave in certain ways and have less choice than we do. A spider doesn't think, 'Hey, I fancy making a really special web today.' It just makes a web because it needs to make a web. A bird doesn't think, 'Hmm, I don't think I'll go to Africa this winter: I fancy a cruise in the Greek Islands and maybe while I'm there I'll learn to windsurf.' No, the weather starts to get cold and the bird just flies in the direction nature makes it fly.

You have to admit that humans can do **MORE** things that other animals can't do. Here are some hugely important things that only humans can do.

- Find a way to survive in all environments – desert, mountains, the Arctic, underwater, space, underground, in trees.
- Understand the way the world works, not just the small part we live in but also parts we've never been to.
- Write information down, so that each generation knows more than the last.
- Produce art, music, stories, poetry.
- Understand what someone else is thinking or meaning – research[14] shows that even the cleverest animals (such as chimpanzees) can only do this about as well as a three to four year-old human. By the time a child is five or six, he or she is way ahead of what other animals can do.
- Invent incredibly complicated things, like computers and aeroplanes, and medical equipment that can see and work inside the human body.
- Think logically, make decisions by thinking about

what might happen, make decisions about what is right or wrong.

So, what's special about the human brain?

Mainly, the cortex. Especially the prefrontal cortex (the bit at the very front of the frontal cortex, just behind your forehead). You've already seen that the whole frontal cortex in a human is bigger than in most other mammals, but you've also seen that size isn't everything. Scientists are still trying to decide exactly what it is that makes our prefrontal cortex work so well. But there's no doubt that it does work well.

Our amazing prefrontal cortex allows us to have social skills, make judgements and decisions, understand the moral of a story, guess what others mean and think, plan ahead and understand future and past, control our emotions, and, very importantly, **NOT** do something that we would like to do.

BRAINY FACTS Though it depends how you measure it, the prefrontal cortex is believed to make up 29% of a human brain but only 3.5% of a cat's.[15] And you thought cats were clever? Well, they are clever at what cats do, but we can do so much more. (Measuring the prefrontal cortex is tricky because it's not easy to see exactly where it ends, and this figure is different according to some researchers.)

I want to highlight two especially important things that

our prefrontal cortex lets us do, which most other animals can't do, or at least not nearly so well (I'll use my dog as an example of an animal).

1 Delaying pleasure

Now, my dog is lovely and (in my opinion) extraordinarily clever. For a dog. She's brilliant at smelling, running, chasing squirrels, and knowing when it's time for her food. She understands a lot of commands and words, and knows how to make my husband give her an extra biscuit.

But, my dog (who happens to be a Labrador and Labradors are famously greedy) cannot delay the pleasure of her meal. Once we allow her to start, it is gone in literally five seconds. On a slow day. When she finishes, she looks around as if to say, 'What? Where did that go?' She's six years and nine months old, and has two meals a day, which means she's had 4,920 meals (or maybe a few more, because she sometimes tells my husband I haven't fed her). Yet, she cannot learn that if she eats more slowly she would have longer pleasure. She might even notice what it tastes like.

2 Predicting the future result of actions

When it comes to predicting the result of her actions and making a decision based on them, my dog is rubbish. She should know by now that if she steals my chocolate biscuit, she'll be in serious trouble. (It's happened before.) So, she sees my chocolate biscuit. Does she think, 'I'm going to be in serious trouble and may not get my dinner if I eat that chocolate biscuit,' and then leave the chocolate biscuit? Er, no. She eats the chocolate biscuit because she doesn't think at all. Useless prefrontal cortex. Zero ability to make decisions based on likely results. She wants the pleasure of the moment, nothing more.

You *MIGHT* say she's making a very sensible decision because she's a hunter and therefore is programmed to go after food, and even that she has **DECIDED** to accept the possible punishment. But I'd say there's been no decision-making at all – she's programmed and she just does it. If I were very cruel and had caused her serious pain when she stole a biscuit before, I suppose she *MIGHT* not steal it again – but that would be through fear of pain, not a real decision. I think it would be her amygdala that was reacting, not her prefrontal cortex. And I wouldn't cause her pain. Trust me, my angry voice is frightening enough for her to know that what she's done is **BAD**. And she knows it's bad – you can tell by her body language – but she still does it because she can't help herself; she can't think it through and take control by making a decision.

A small human child doesn't have a good prefrontal cortex either, and so may well steal that chocolate biscuit. But human children learn – their brains develop and they soon reach an age when they can

DECIDE whether to take the risk. Dogs don't. They just eat. Dogs may be cleverer than worms and hippopotamuses – and a lot more cuddly and wonderful – but their prefrontal cortex is not in our league. And even though chimpanzees can learn to do amazing things, they simply don't have a prefrontal cortex that would let them do half of what you can do.

You may be interested to know that being able to delay pleasure is something that many psychologists now believe is very important for success in life. An example would be to say, 'I won't eat that chocolate now, but I'll save it till later because I'll enjoy it more and deserve it later.' But how can delaying chocolate mean success in later life? Well, it's all about putting future pleasure before immediate pleasure, which involves planning and considering the future, and it's all wrapped up in ambition, decision-making and control. You need those things for success in later life. But before you can have those things, you need a good prefrontal cortex.

One study in the US showed that pupils' self-control and ability to delay pleasure was a better way of predicting whether they would be successful at school than a normal intelligence test such as an IQ test.[16] And since you can improve any skill, if you try to improve your self-control and say **NO** to things you want to do sometimes, you could be developing your brain in a very positive way indeed. Each time you do it, think about your brain learning to make good decisions.

Don't say no all the time, though – there's nothing wrong with having pleasure sometimes. In fact, it's very important.

> **BRAINY FACT** from the animal world: the Australian anteater has a massive frontal cortex. Much bigger than a human one. Are Australian anteaters geniuses? No. Australian anteaters are stupendously thick at everything except ant-eating. So, what went wrong? Well, they have a pathetically small limbic system. The moral of the story is that to be clever and effective you have to have a great frontal cortex AND a good limbic system, working in harmony. Nothing wrong with being emotional – in fact, it could be the key to success.

So, all brains are amazing, but human brains top the bill in terms of learning abilities. And it's all down to:

1 our thick, well developed cortex, especially our large frontal and prefrontal cortexes;

2 how the cortex works together with the other parts of the brain, including the limbic system. And the limbic system loves chocolate biscuits...

This book will make your brain even better than it is now. While you read and **ENJOY** reading each chapter, and while you feel good about the new things you are learning, your cortex and your limbic system are both developing and strengthening.

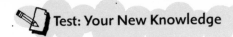

Test: Your New Knowledge

- Remember, you can look back and find the answers.
- Write answers in your notebook/on a piece of paper.
- Spend a few minutes learning them.
- Then get someone to test you.

1 The two halves of your brain are called the right and left _____.

2 The part of your brain that controls breathing is the _____.

3 The word 'cerebellum' means _____.

4 The parts that mostly deal with emotion are found in the _____.

5 The part most important for memory and learning is the _____.

6 The _____ is where fear and anger start.

7 Which half of the human brain usually deals with language?

8 How much of the human brain does the prefrontal cortex occupy?

9 How much of a cat's brain does the prefrontal cortex occupy?

10 What is one important thing that my dog's brain does not allow her to do?

Time for a **BRAIN BOOST** – choose any two from pages 187–192.

Chapter 4

HEALTHY BRAIN

Care for your brain ~ Fuel your brain ~ Water your brain ~ Air your brain ~ Rest your brain ~ Happy brain ~ Interested brain

Care for your brain

All brains are different in some ways but they all need the same things to be healthy. Some things are definitely good for brains. There are others that scientists haven't completely agreed about. And some things are definitely bad for our brains.

Writing this chapter made me change my habits. I thought I already had a good diet, but I soon realized I was missing some clever, interesting and easy ways to make my brain work better. I felt that if I was going to tell you what's good for you, I should follow that advice myself. So I did. And look how brainy I became!

Of course, I don't know if I became brainier, but I do know three things that changed **IMMEDIATELY**:

! I wasn't hungry between meals any more.
! I didn't feel sleepy in the afternoons and I
   could concentrate for ages.
! And, amazingly, I didn't want sugary things.

> **BRAINY TIP** You will sometimes read weird and wonderful (and sometimes plain weird) stuff about what is good or bad for you – especially on the internet. Don't believe everything you read. For this chapter, I've been careful to use the best scientific material, supported by recognized experts; I have ignored claims by companies trying to sell things, unless already backed by good university research. When something's interesting but there's not much evidence yet, I have said so. And if something seems to go against all the other research, I have ignored it.

Fuel your brain

Your brain never stops working. Even when you are asleep, it's still working. It needs fuel to keep going, just like the rest of your body. We get our energy from food – called **calories**. When you run, you use more energy/calories than when you are sitting still.

Your brain uses a lot of energy even though it just seems to sit there. In fact, although your brain is only 2 percent of your whole body weight, it uses a massive 20 percent of the energy your whole body uses.

Hmm – does that mean that if I do some maths (the most difficult thing for **MY** brain), I can eat lots of chocolate and not get fat? I could even get to like maths if that's true... Unfortunately, it's not, as you will find out. Chocolate is not what keeps our brains working well. Which is a real shame.

Your brain is fussy and wants the right foods, at the

right times. Otherwise, it can't work properly. You may feel dizzy, cross, or tired; you may find it hard to concentrate and remember; you may even behave badly. (Surely not!)

But it's so easy to eat food that will make your brain and body work well. You never need be hungry. And it's delicious food too – not weird or horrible. Even if you're a picky eater, you will find healthy foods that you like – and you will grow to like them even better if you keep choosing them.

Healthy eating is not about following boring rules. It's about real enjoyment of delicious food. It's about feeling strong, well, and full of energy.

Take control in the kitchen

You may think you have no control over what you eat, because someone else buys the food and chooses the meals. Let me tell you a secret: whoever buys your food would be **DELIGHTED** if you showed an interest. They may be *DYING* for someone to think up new ideas for meals. And I bet they don't know a lot of the info in this chapter.

Try this: find an adult and say, 'Do we have any **choline**-rich foods in the house?' The adult will say either, 'What?' or 'Why?' Answer, 'My brain needs choline to work well.' By the end of this chapter, you will know what these foods are for.

You could even make your parents brainier. Maybe you don't want them to be brainier – after all, parents are pretty know-it-all already. But imagine: if their brains work better, they will do better in their jobs; then they could earn more money; and then the whole family will be better off. Just think: if you are the one who makes their brains work better, they will be for ever grateful to you. A very happy position for you.

Healthy eating

The key to a healthy brain and body is variety. Even with the healthiest foods, if you eat too much of one item or food from only one group, this would not be a good diet.

The great news is that you need never be hungry because you can fill up on a wide variety from the different groups.

IMPORTANT POINT Although many people are overweight, many are not. It's also dangerous to be too thin. So, although low-fat yogurts or other products are right for most people, they are not if you need to put on weight. If you are not sure whether you are a healthy weight, ask a qualified person, such as a GP or dietician.

The British Nutrition Foundation has devised something called the Balance of Good Health model. You may have learned about it in school. It shows how any type of food can be part of a healthy diet. Foods are divided into five groups, and shown as a picture of a dinner plate with different sized sections, depending on how much of each you should eat as part of your diet. If you want to see more details, go to **www.nutrition.org.uk**.

I have followed their advice and here is how I explain it. The first two groups are where you should find most of your food; the third and fourth groups are the next most important; and the fifth group should form only a small part of your diet.

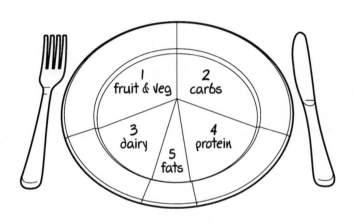

1 **fruit and veg — for fibre, vitamins, minerals, anti-oxidants, and energy — eat lots**

Choose a variety of any fruit and veg, including a range of different colours, from dark green to bright yellow, orange, red and purple. Especially remember dark green, which will mean the food is high in folate, something many young people lack.

2 Carbohydrates and whole grains – for energy, fibre, minerals, B vitamins and some protein – eat lots, for good energy throughout the day

Rice (especially brown), pasta (especially wholegrain), seeded/multigrain wholemeal bread, potatoes (especially new potatoes and especially potatoes with their skins on), wholegrain cereals (not sugar-or honey-coated), **fortified** cereals (good source of iron), porridge.

3 Milk and dairy foods – for protein and calcium; these foods also give energy

Milk, cheese, yogurt, soya milk/desserts fortified with calcium. Choose reduced fat varieties of milk and yogurt – but not if you are underweight.

4 Meat, fish and vegetarian alternatives – providing protein, essential for growth, repair, energy and many nutrients

Chicken, fish, red meat (avoid fatty parts), eggs (egg yolk also contains iron), beans, lentils, nuts, tofu, soya, dairy foods (especially choose lower fat varieties).

5 Fats and sugars – fats contain some essential nutrients and sugar provides energy; both should only be eaten in small amounts

Oily fish, olive/sunflower/rapeseed/flaxseed/grapeseed and canola oils, walnut and other nut oils (unless you have an allergy). As for sugars, see below.

VEGETARIAN? Or Vegan? If so, you will need to get protein and other essentials from other sources – such as nuts, beans and pulses (and eggs and dairy food if you are not vegan). If you are already vegetarian or vegan you probably know how to do this. There are also books, websites and organizations to help you. Before becoming vegetarian or vegan, take steps to learn about it. Never limit your diet unless someone such as a registered dietician shows you how to get the right nutrients.

Are some sugars better than others?

Sugars are very complicated. You find them naturally in fruit, vegetables and milk, for example – where they are an excellent way to get energy. But sugars can also be added to things, often in large quantities: try to keep all *added* sugars to a minimum. Sucrose, glucose, dextrose, maltose, honey and syrup are all forms of added sugar. Start reading food labels.

Are some fats better than others?

We need some fat in our diet but it should be the right type – the brain needs the right fats to keep it working.

Cut down on **saturated** fat – found especially in fatty meat, the skin of chicken and poultry, processed meats such as burgers and sausages and factory-made meat pies, lots of supermarket ready meals, many cakes and biscuits, pastries, and cream, butter, full-fat cheese and milk, coconut, coconut cream and palm oil. Red meat with a very small amount of fat is fine as part of a varied diet – and is a good source of iron.

The worst fats are **trans-fatty** acids or **trans-fats**. (The label may say 'partially hydrogenated' or 'hydrogenated' fat.) Try to avoid these completely. Research suggests that eating too many may cause learning problems (though it's not yet proven) and may interfere with your brain's ability to send messages.[17] Some countries ban them.

'Unsaturated' fats are healthier – both **monounsaturated** and **polyunsaturated**. They will be labelled on the packaging. But don't add large amounts of these to your food in cooking or dressings, because they are also found in some fruit, veg and nuts, as well as in spreading fats.

The healthiest fats are called **omega oils** – especially omega-3 and omega-6. The best source is oily fish – such as fresh or canned mackerel, salmon, sardines, herring, kippers, trout and fresh tuna (not tinned) – and certain vegetable oils, especially flaxseed, walnut, sunflower and canola, as well as rapeseed, grapeseed and soy. Use them in cooking where needed and your brain will thank you!

There's growing evidence that omega-3 is important for brain development. In a recent study, about 40 per cent of the children improved in schoolwork after taking omega-3 fish oils in a capsule.[18] BUT, this does not mean that supplements are a good idea: the children who improved may have had a poor diet before. In fact, the pupils who had learning difficulties, *and* a diet that lacked essential oils, were the ones who seemed to benefit from extra omega-3. If your diet is good, you don't need supplements.

Vitamins are destroyed at high temperatures and oils lose their value. For stir-frying, choose grapeseed, olive or canola, which can manage higher temperatures. But never overheat any oil – when they start to smoke, they lose their healthiness.

> **BRAINY TIP** Flaxseed oil is high in healthy omega oils, **BUT** personally I think it tastes of oily fish, which is fine if you are cooking oily fish, but foul if you are frying an egg or stir-frying veg. Some people love it though, so don't let me put you off. My favourites are grapeseed, rapeseed and canola – these are cheap and tasty.

Do I need vitamin and mineral pills?

Not if you eat properly. Most experts say that our bodies absorb vitamins and minerals better from food than from pills and potions. High intakes of some vitamins and minerals can be dangerous, perhaps especially for young people. It's cheaper, tastier, safer and almost certainly better to build a healthy brain and body through delicious and healthy foods.

Or herbal supplements that claim to make my brain better?

No. There's no good reason for young people to take them. Not enough research has been done into their safety, especially for children. Much of the research has been done on animals, not humans.

Super brainy foods

Eating a good variety of the above foods is the way to a healthy lifestyle. But there are some foods that seem to be extra good for brains – though in certain cases more research is needed.

However good they are, you still need to combine them with lots of other healthy foods. In other words, though oily fish is great for brains, this does **NOT** mean that if you only eat oily fish you'll become a genius.

After all, eating oily fish hasn't done much for sharks. Perhaps they should eat blueberries too. And walnuts...

Egg yolk and soya – especially for their high choline content, which may be useful for memory and concentration. You also need foods rich in **folic acid** – e.g. dark-green leafy veg – to help your body process choline.

Oily fish – for example, sardine, salmon, mackerel, pilchard – for its high levels of the essential omega oils, including omega-3. If you don't like the idea of whole fish, try mashing tinned salmon or pilchards or smoked mackerel into a pâté with a bit of lemon juice and some low-fat cream cheese. (There's nothing wrong with tinned tuna, by the way – just that it loses its omega richness. For some reason, other tinned fish are still omega-rich. Tinned tuna is good for you for its protein content, but doesn't count as oily fish.)

Whole grains and fruit and veg – for their slow-release carbohydrates, giving your brain a steady flow of energy through the day. Porridge is one of the best breakfast foods for this reason. Try to have some whole grains and fruit or veg with every meal.

Protein (but not fatty meats) – I have to say there's a bit of an argument about protein. We know it is important in many ways: it gives energy, helps build and repair cells and also helps the brain produce the **neurotransmitters** that keep it working effectively. Many people say that protein in a meal or snack is the key to keeping your brain working, and stops you feeling hungry between meals. But most diet experts focus on wholegrain carbohydrates and say that this is what gives you energy for a long period. I would definitely follow their advice, **BUT** I personally find that if I do not include enough protein in a meal as well, I am hungry half an hour later. Or sleepy. And often both!

The main change I made to my diet when I started writing *Know Your Brain* was to eat more protein with my carbs – such as beans with my breakfast, chicken or tuna with my lunch, and yogurt with both – and it really keeps my brain awake and full of energy. Maybe I was just eating too little protein before?

We do have to be careful about choosing protein though, as it can have a high fat content – often saturated fat. And it's certainly right that most of our food should be from the first two groups on page 59.

Brazil nuts – and other nuts – for selenium, which is important for brain function. Especially useful for vegetarians because another main source of selenium is meat. Nuts are also a good source of protein and many different nutrients. They are great energy foods – ever wondered how squirrels run up and down trees all day?

Whole grains, green leafy veg, fortified cereals, beans, Marmite, Vegemite – for vitamin B, which regulates mood and brain performance; and other nutrients important for brains.

Dark-green leafy veg, egg yolk or red meat – for iron. Not having enough iron can make a big difference to brain function and concentration.

Yogurt – for its **tyrosine** content, which some people believe perks the brain up. This is *not* proven, and it may be nothing to do with tyrosine, but I am including it because I personally find that eating a yogurt after lunch and/or breakfast is a really good way of keeping me awake and not hungry. This could simply be the protein, of course, or even the carbohydrate. Whichever, it's good news! It solves my problem of often wanting something sweet at the end of a meal. Added to that, it's an important source of calcium, to help bones and nails. I choose low-fat because I do not need to put on weight. Avoid added sugar if possible – ideally, have plain yogurt and add fruit and/or seeds.

Strawberries and blueberries – for their antioxidants. Some scientists found that these fruits gave rats better memory, co-ordination and concentration.[19] Another study showed that food full of antioxidants helped the learning abilities of dogs.[20] (Maybe I should give my dog some blueberries…) We can't be sure it's the same for humans, of course, but antioxidants are believed to be good for the brain and general health. Other research shows that some of the best places to find antioxidants are in apples, strawberries, raspberries, cranberries, blueberries and kidney beans.[21] Not dog food.

Colour – it's often the bright colours that give the goodness to fruit and veg, so think of rainbows and go for as many colours as possible. Try cranberries, blueberries, strawberries, carrots, oranges, spinach, peas, red peppers and tomatoes. The stronger the colour, the better – as long as you are not thinking about artificial colours. Skittles and Smarties are not full of goodness – sorry.

Seeds – no, not the ones designed for gardens. Edible pumpkin, sunflower and sesame seeds, for example, are full of minerals and vitamins, as well as fibre. And they taste great.

- Sprinkle them on salads, soups and in stir-fries.
- Have fun with sprouting seeds – mung beans, alfalfa and bean sprouts, all available from health food shops and some supermarkets. You just rinse a few and put them in a clean glass jar on a windowsill; rinse them once a day and watch them grow. When they've all sprouted, eat them! Perhaps the freshest food you've ever eaten, and stuffed with goodness. Feel your brain smile.

NOT TRUE Many people say that turkey and hot milk make you sleepy because they are high in tryptophan. This is quite possibly a myth.

Adults probably feel sleepy after their Christmas meal because they've eaten and drunk too much; and you may fall asleep after a night-time drink of hot milk because .... it's night-time!

Brainy meal tips

Breakfast – research proves that we perform better all day when we eat a good breakfast.[22] Some research also shows that children who eat sugary drinks and snacks at breakfast work less well.[23]

- ✪ ***Smart breakfast choices*** – add a drink of milk to any of these:
  - baked beans on wholegrain toast;
  - porridge + yogurt/fruit;
  - wholegrain toast + Marmite + a yogurt;
  - two boiled/scrambled eggs + toast;
  - wholewheat pancakes topped with banana + yogurt;
  - peanut butter on a wholegrain bagel or roll;
  - fortified breakfast cereal and home-made milkshake (instead of milk drink) – blend semi-skimmed milk with a banana and/or any berries; add a dessertspoonful of wheatgerm;

Snacks – snack sensibly: don't let yourself get hungry, but don't use sugar to deal with hunger. Avoid processed cakes, biscuits and pastries – try my Brain cakes (recipe on page 191), home-made flapjacks, carrot cake or banana bread made with wholemeal flour.

- ✪ ***Smart snacks include:***
  - any fruit / dried fruit – almost every fruit you can think of comes in a dried variety – delicious;
  - cheese/low-fat cream cheese and crackers/

oatcakes;
- small cheese, egg or tinned salmon sandwich with wholegrain bread;
- breadsticks or bagel and low-fat cream cheese;
- any nuts and seeds;
- low-fat yogurt;
- wholegrain currant buns;
- avocado dip or hummus with carrots;
- slice of brain cake – go on: you know you want one!

Lunches – lunch should contain protein, carbohydrate, veg/fruit and dairy.

✪ ***Smart lunches*** – add a piece of fruit and/or a yogurt if hungry:
- tuna/chicken/egg/cheese sandwich (wholegrain bread) + tomato + celery + sugar snap peas;
- omelette with tomato + pepper + green leaf salad, home-made carrot or banana cake;
- pasta/couscous with fresh tuna/chicken, raw spinach + tomato salad, with grated carrot;
- baked potato with cheese and baked beans/ tuna/sardines + salad;
- lentil soup + wholegrain roll + cottage cheese + carrot sticks;
- chicken/fish with rice or potatoes and any green veg;

Time for a **BRAIN** 💡 **BOOST** – choose a banana/other fruit/raisins/nuts/seeds, or a sandwich with wholegrain, seeded bread, and a drink.

Water your brain

Your brain is more than 70 per cent water. It needs plenty of water to work well.

Although everyone agrees that we should drink water, not everyone agrees about the details. Some people say it must be plain water and that juice or tea or milk don't have the same benefits. But water is a large part of **ALL** liquids – and is a major part of foods as well. For example, an apple is more than 90 per cent water and fish is around 70 per cent water.

Some people say you should drink water with meals; others that you should drink it separately from meals or that you should drink mineral water; others say tap water is the best. Some say it should be filtered. Well, they can't all be right, can they?

Sorry, I am supposed to be telling you to drink water – and *YES, WATER IS VERY GOOD FOR YOU!* – but now I seem to be telling you not to believe everything you hear. Because thinking carefully, researching things, keeping an open mind, and not believing everything without question, are all also good for your brain.

What happens if you don't have enough liquid?

Being dehydrated affects your concentration. Some research shows that children performed worse at maths when they had too little water.[24] And a school in the north of England noticed great improvements in behaviour and learning ability after staff stopped children drinking fizzy drinks and gave them water instead.[25] The results were so clear that other schools joined a campaign to encourage children to drink more water.

How much is enough?

Experts say that you get more than a third of your water needs from the food you eat. Apart from food, you should also drink six to eight glasses of non-sugary, non-alcoholic fluid spread out during a day, and more on a hot day or if you exercise vigorously.

Don't overdo it: it's dangerous (though difficult) to drink much **TOO** much water. There have been cases of marathon runners thinking they have to drink far more than they really need: at the London Marathon in 2003, fourteen runners had to be taken to hospital with dangerous levels of water in their bodies, described as 'water on the brain'. They had serious symptoms. One said he had drunk thirteen litres in five hours, but the advice, especially for beginners and slower runners, is to drink about half a litre each hour of a run. The next year, runners had better advice and only one runner had problems.

A POSSIBLE MYTH? I read a report saying that teenage boys aged 14+ may need more water – but this goes against wider expert advice. Boys of that age often eat more, and there's water in food, remember. And they may play a lot of sport, so will naturally drink a bit extra then, too. Boys of 14+ should follow the same advice as everyone else. Drink enough, within normal recommendations, and relax.

Brain says yes!

Your brain will work well with these drinks:

Water

- *Tap water* – if you live in a place with a clean water supply, tap water is the ideal drink.

NOTE: don't drink water from a bathroom tap or hot tap – this may have sat around in a tank for days/weeks/months. Your kitchen tap is connected directly to the water supply, and this is safe to drink from. Drinking fountains also contain good water.

- *There's no need for bottled water* – it's expensive and unnecessary.

AND: some people say that the minerals in some

bottled water may be harmful.

AND: recently there was a scare about plastic bottles, with a fear that chemicals could pass into the water. Plastic's worse for the environment too. So much to worry about!

Fresh juice – a good way to increase liquid intake. The fruit sugars will give you a little more energy than plain water, and a small amount of fibre too. But don't drink too much: it can be bad for your teeth, so drink water afterwards, or clean your teeth – but wait at least half an hour before cleaning them, as your saliva helps deal with the fruit acid. Juice is expensive, too. Try diluting it. And best to drink it with a meal rather than in between.

Diluted squashes – if you choose ones that are low in sugar, these are fine in moderation. But they're not as good as water, and worse for your teeth.

Tea – there's no proof it helps your brain (though some people swear by green tea as long as you don't add milk) but a moderate amount of tea is a good way to keep fluids up.

Tea contains **caffeine** – see info on coffee on page 76.

Fruit teas are a great idea. There are lots of different flavours so even if you don't like one, you may love another.

Milk – milk is really more a food than a drink because it contains protein and other nutrients. Semi-skimmed is recommended for most people over the age of two. Full-cream has more fat, and is suitable for those who need to put on weight. Skimmed and semi-skimmed contain more calcium but less of vitamins A and D – but if you're eating properly you will have plenty of those from other foods.

Brain says no!

Your brain will not thank you for these drinks so don't drink them:

Sugary drinks, including some diluting squashes – research suggests that brains do not work well with sudden rushes of sugar[26] and you'd be amazed how much sugar is in many brands of drinks. Original Ribena, for example, contains 60 grams of sugar in a 500 ml portion. A normal ten-year-old should only have 50–60 grams of sugar in a whole day.[27]

Performance-enhancing drinks – not the best way to give your brain regular energy. They contain masses of sugar: 500ml of Lucozade Energy has over 80 grams of sugar, for example. They are designed for people doing heavy sport and will give you a sudden energy rush that will not last long and then your body will demand fuel again: if you are not doing a lot of physical activity, you should choose other drinks.

fizzy drinks – fizzy drinks, such as cola and other popular drinks, are full of sugar and other chemicals, which don't help your brain. Your mood and energy levels will go up and down a lot; you may be fidgety and stressed.

What about low-sugar/low-calorie? Bad idea: one of the main **artificial sweeteners**, aspartame, seems to be linked with behaviour and learning problems in some people, though this isn't proven. Fizzy drinks are also bad for your teeth.

The clear message is: cut right back on fizzy drinks (except perhaps fizzy water with pure fruit juice) if you want your brain to work well.

fast-food/artificial milkshakes – often full of horrible trans-fats, sugar, artificial sweeteners and chemicals. Say no!

Coffee – although the caffeine in coffee (and tea and hot chocolate) can keep you awake and alert for a while, the effect doesn't last and there are better ways to achieve it. Caffeine can be addictive and when you have too much it can make you jumpy, anxious and irritable; it can give you headaches too. The best way to have an alert brain is to have enough food, water and sleep.

Alcohol – the worst drink for the brain. Although adults can have some other health benefits from small amounts of alcohol, it always makes the brain work less well. Alcohol relaxes your brain and makes you feel you can do things better than you can. And when children and teenagers drink alcohol, the brain is very easily damaged – often permanently. Being drunk kills brain cells. Dead.

In short

So, the message is that we need water, but that it can (and does) come from the foods and other drinks that we consume. Avoid added sugar and sweeteners, cut down on the fizzy drinks, and don't overdo it on the caffeine. Other than that, drink your six to eight glasses – with extra in hot weather or when exercising – in whatever form you like.

Cheers!

Time for a **BRAIN BOOST** – a drink, of course!
Tea? Water? Juice? Milk? Or choose a boost
from page 190

Air your brain

Well, of course we all need air. But this is about that most important part of the air: oxygen. Our brains need lots of oxygen to work.

But how do you get more oxygen to your brain?

Exercise

- Oxygen is carried to your brain in your blood. And blood gets moving more when your body gets moving.

- It doesn't have to be exhausting – you don't have to sweat or get out of breath. Walking is enough – so walk, whenever you can.

- In fact, although really hard exercise is good for your body, it's not the best thing to do just before you want to do brainy stuff.

- Tips for exercise...
  - Walk instead of getting the bus.
  - Take the stairs instead of the lift.
  - **RUN** up the stairs instead of walk.
  - Go for a cycle ride.
  - Get up from your desk and do some star jumps or running on the spot for a minute. Get those knees high! (Don't do it in the middle of class.)
  - Try to walk 10,000 steps a day – you can get a cheap step-counter (a pedometer) which you attach to your belt and it counts every step you take. Even walking to the fridge counts. Knowing that your steps are being counted actually makes you walk more steps – I've done it, so I know...

BRAINY FACT Scientists believe that exercise may actually make brains grow new neurons – and also may even help repair damage.[28] They don't say how much exercise is necessary to do this but the

mice that were studied had to run rather a lot... The scientists think that any exercise is better than none, and that the more you can do the better. One study showed that mice who used a running wheel regularly for six weeks were better at learning new tasks than mice that had no way of exercising.[29]

Breathe well

- ✪ Lots of people don't. When you breathe properly, your stomach should move in and out, not the top of your chest. Relax your stomach muscles and breathe from lower down.
- ✪ Every now and then, take a break from what you're doing, stand up, swing your arms around and take some deep breaths (again, not in the middle of class).
- ✪ Have a window open. If you spend too much time in a closed room, or in a room with lots of other people, you end up with less oxygen. You (and everyone else) breathe **IN** oxygen and breathe **OUT** carbon dioxide. So, gradually, the room has more carbon dioxide and less oxygen. You won't suffocate but you will have worse concentration and may get headaches. Not good for your brain.

Get outside

- ✪ Even if it's raining. You should get at least half an hour of fresh air every day, and preferably much more. You'll be amazed how much more energy you have and how much better you work.

Can I buy oxygen?

✪ Why would you, when it's free? But there are such things as oxygen bars, where people go and have a drink and buy a canister of oxygen to breathe. Experts don't agree on whether there's any point, though some research suggests that it helped surgical patients fight infection.[30]

But it's not cheap and young people can't go in bars anyway! You're not missing anything: you'd be better going outside for a walk with the dog, kicking a football or going to the park with your friends.

Time for a **BRAIN BOOST** – run up and down the stairs. And again! Or choose one from page 187–190

Rest your brain

Our brains can't work so well if we don't have enough sleep. Memory, concentration, accuracy, alertness, maths and logic all suffer.

✪ Parents of babies know how lack of sleep makes them feel. Gritty-eyed. Dopey. And very grumpy.

✪ When researchers gave people an extra hour of sleep, they did better on learning and memory tasks.[31]

✪ Losing too much sleep can make you as useless as a drunk person.

But that's not all. The brain does remarkable things while asleep: it practises what you were doing during the day. That's brilliant: I sleep, my brain gets better.

- ❂ When scientists scanned the brains of sleeping people, they saw that the same brain cells were active as were active before they slept. This seems to work for all sorts of things: solving problems, practising musical instruments, learning facts and figures, playing computer games. If you play a musical instrument, you might have had the experience of struggling with a piece and then finding that the next day you can suddenly do it better. Your brilliant brain has been working while you were asleep.

- ❂ Scientists examined the brains of cats and found that cats that were allowed to sleep for six hours after a learning task showed greater brain changes than cats that had not slept.[32]

- ❂ If you have a test, read over your notes the evening before, then go to sleep at a sensible time. This is much better than staying up late learning for the test.

- ❂ Having a nap after you've done some work could help you remember it. Definitely not recommended at school.

SLEEPY FACT People can have incredibly brilliant ideas just as they are coming out of sleep. There was a famous Russian chemist called Mendeleev – who discovered the periodic table of chemical elements, (something that I NEVER understood) – and he said he discovered it in a dream.

Actually, I sometimes have brilliant ideas in my sleep. Unfortunately, I forget them when I wake up.

Tips for good sleeping

⊗ During the hour before bedtime, avoid:
- fizzy drinks, coffee, tea;
- exercise that makes your heart rate rise or your breathing speed up;
- excitement – e.g. a frightening film;
- video or computer games; the internet and instant messaging – especially if you are having an argument with someone;
- bright lights and loud music;
- stress and shouting;
- a large meal.

⊗ During the hour before bedtime, do:
- drink hot milk/cocoa;
- eat a carbohydrate snack: bread, milk, cereal – not just before sleep, but an hour before;
- write down a list of things you want to remember tomorrow, and read over it;
- say something nice to someone – it'll make you

feel good;

- In a room burner (if you have one and are allowed to use it) heat a few drops of lavender or geranium oil mixed with water. Or sprinkle some on your pillow;
- read or listen to **GENTLE** music;
- think about the good things that happened during the day;
- read something funny, to relax you. Or something really, really boring, to send you to sleep.

Time for a **BRAIN BOOST** – lie flat on the floor with your eyes shut. Let your body relax completely. Breathe slowly. Stay like that for several minutes, just thinking about your breathing.

Happy brain

We learn better when we are relaxed, positive and happy. Stress stops your brain working at its best. The trouble is, it's not always easy to be relaxed, especially in a classroom or when faced with work we find difficult.

Some of the tips below won't work when you're in school. On the other hand, you could get together with some friends and discuss all this with your teachers – they will probably be very happy to try to find ways that will help your learning and concentration.

Your brain loves to laugh

When you laugh and smile, the muscles that you use to smile trigger happy chemicals in your brain – and research has shown that you don't even have to THINK it's funny – just grin anyway. So – preferably when no one is looking – smile. Or treat yourself to a funny programme, film or book before you work.

Your brain loves to love

One great way to give your brain love is to have a pet animal. Lots of studies show that caring for a pet reduces stress and raises happiness. It helps depression and can even help people in hospital to recover.

So, if you have a dog or cat, go and play a game with it. Or if it's an ancient, grumpy cat that doesn't want to play, stroke it. It doesn't have to be a dog or a cat – hamsters, guinea pigs and rabbits can all have the same effect.

I don't think I'd add spiders or cockroaches to the list. You can't stroke or play with them. Yes, I know, some people stroke spiders, but they are **STRANGE** people.

Research has shown that when people stroke an animal, their **blood pressure** goes down, their heart rate slows, and their body produces chemicals called **endorphins**, which are nature's painkillers. And some studies have shown that you don't even need to stroke it – even having a dog in the room while you work helps. Even watching a tank full of fish can lower blood pressure. Or send you to sleep...

But remember – a dog is for life, and not just for homework.

I must say, my dog (you know, the one who steals chocolate biscuits – except that of course I don't **EAT** chocolate biscuits now because they don't help my brain and I don't want them) is at this moment lying asleep, curled in her bed beside my desk, and when I look at her I do get a very happy 'ahhhh' feeling.

Until she starts staring at me and whining to go for a walk...

Your brain loves nature

The natural environment, such as a garden, woods, or a beautiful natural view, can be really good for stress, blood pressure and brain activity.[33]

Tips for using your brain's need for nature

- If you have a nice view out of your window, place your desk so you can see it.
- If you don't have a nice view, get a lovely picture of an outdoor scene and put it where you can see it easily.
- Grow a plant – on a windowsill or in a pot inside your room; start a window box; grow sprouting seeds (see page 68).
- If somewhere near you is foul with litter, or if your garden is a mess, clear it up/weed it. (Before you

clear litter in a public place, check with an adult as there may be safety issues.)

- Go to your nearest park, trees, open space, and just look at it; breathe deeply; appreciate it.
- Get as much daylight as you can. Research also shows that this helps mood and wakefulness.[34]
- Work outside when you can.
- Do some conservation work at weekends – good for you and the environment.

Be good to yourself – especially when you have work to do.

- Reward yourself often. Tell yourself that once you have learnt/written/read the next section/page/exercise, you can have a brain boost or a rest or a small treat of your choice. Even chocolate occasionally – although it's not exactly the perfect brain food, it gives pleasure and is fine every now and then. Pleasure is not a bad thing.
- Praise yourself – your limbic system loves praise. Feel proud of what you have just done, however small it was.
- Feeling in control will help you feel happy – and following the tips in this book will help you be in control.
- If things are upsetting you, imagine a cupboard inside your head, and put those bad thoughts inside it. Don't open the cupboard door while you are working.

✪ When doing a subject you hate, or that you find hard, ask yourself: 'Why am I doing this? What will I gain from it?' If your answer is negative – such as, 'Goodness knows! I haven't a clue. I am **NEVER** going to use this stuff **EVER** again in my whole life. I mean, why on earth am I learning poetry when I want to be a scientist?' – then you will be grumpy and unhappy and will *NOT* learn it easily. BUT, if you find a better answer – such as, 'Because it will make me feel good if I can manage it. Because I will get good marks and find it easier to succeed at school. Because my teacher/mum/dad/grandpa will be pleased with me. Because I am clever enough. Because everything I can do will make my brain better,' – then you WILL find it easier.

BRAINY TIP – FENG SHUI

The space/room where you work and sleep can change your mood. Have you heard of feng shui?[35] It is all about arranging your space so that you can work well and feel better. For example, feng shui principles say you should not work with a door behind you. Whether you believe that or not, see if anything makes you feel tense in the room where you work. Your desk might feel too close to something, or your chair too low, or the position of your mirror may mean you keep seeing yourself. That would certainly put me off...

For me, an untidy room would be bad feng shui –

if you think an untidy room is getting you down, there's only one answer. No, don't ask your mum or dad to tidy it – tidy it yourself.

What about a change of colour scheme? Different colours can affect mood. Do you LIKE the colour of your room? If you don't, it could be dragging you down. Can you change it?

Interested brain

Your brain loves new experiences. They give it a kickstart, increase your energy, make you alert. Your brain also likes variety – it doesn't like doing the same thing over and over again. It gets bored easily.

In fact, biology has made your brain like new things and get bored by too much repetition. We would be pretty unsuccessful if we just lay around doing the same thing every day. Wanting new experiences makes us ambitious, makes us experiment, makes us brave. Those are things that make humans successful – otherwise we'd still be sitting around in caves.

Sometimes, though, it's scary trying something new. What if we fail? What if we don't like it? What if our friends are better at it than we are? What if we hurt ourselves? What if we look silly?

Luckily, your brain contains something very clever that makes it want new experiences, even if they are a bit scary. It's sometimes called the pleasure-reward system: when you try something new or exciting, your brain floods with the chemical **dopamine**.

Dopamine gives a feeling of excitement, thrill, satisfaction. Dopamine is also essential for alertness and concentration. It puts the zing in your life. And it helps you learn. In fact, without dopamine you can't learn because you won't be bothered with anything.

So, keep your brain happy by giving it what it most wants: a new sensation.

BRAINY TIP When you are revising, mix new facts in with the old. Interesting research shows that new information makes your brain produce dopamine, making you alert and better able to learn and remember.[36] So, every now and then, find a new fact (anything interesting – even an unusual word in a dictionary) and learn it before going back to your work.

Here are some ways to give your brain new sensations:

- listen to different music. Maybe something classical, or folk, or anything that's not your usual taste;
- challenge yourself by cooking the evening meal for your family;
- learn the words to a song;
- learn the words to a song backwards;
- write a letter with the hand you normally don't write with;
- use your knife and fork in the 'wrong' hands;
- taste something you've never tasted before;

- get a dictionary and learn one new word every day – and try to use it during the day;
- start a new hobby or sport; or start collecting something;
- research spontaneous human combustion – and decide whether you believe in it;
- draw a picture with your eyes shut;
- go to an art gallery. They're usually free. You don't have to look at every picture – go as fast or slowly as you want;
- rearrange the furniture in your room (and be embarrassed by the dust under your bed).

Test: Your New Knowledge of Healthy Brains

First, find something that smells nice. And strong. If you are allowed a scented candle, this would be good – but ASK, or I'll be in trouble. Or it could be an orange peeled and cut into pieces (which you can eat as you do the task). Or a lemon cut up. Or some perfume on a tissue.

Then, find the answers to these questions. All the answers are in this chapter (and you might remember some of them without looking). As you write the answer, **SNIFF** the lovely smell.

1 Name two foods that are rich sources of choline.
2 Children performed better at school when they stopped drinking _____.
3 Which artificial sweetener is linked to behaviour problems?
4 What is the worst drink for the brain?
5 How much of your energy does your brain use?
6 Name three foods that are great sources of 'good' fats.
7 What is the name of the essential fatty acid found in oily fish?
8 What were the two fruits that scientists found improved rats' learning powers?
9 Which ingredient of yogurt may help you stay alert?

10 How much of your brain is made of water?

11 How can you make more oxygen go to your brain?

12 What is the chemical in your brain that gives you a feeling of excitement and pleasure?

13 Find three things that you should avoid before you go to sleep.

14 Name two good sources of iron in food.

Now check your answers. Make any corrections if necessary.

Spend a couple of minutes learning the answers (keep sniffing your smelly object). **BUT** add this new fact as you do it: my dog's name is Amber.

Then, cover the page and either get someone to test you, or write the answers down on a separate piece of paper – and if you get stuck, try sniffing the smell again to see if it triggers the answer.

Proud of yourself? You should be. How many of those could you have answered before you read this chapter? You have learned loads of new facts and now your brain is even better than it was.

A rainbow of fruit and veg

Remember how it's good to eat fruit and veg of all different colours? Well, can you think of some? Think of at least one for each of these – but they must be natural, not full of artificial colouring:

Red
Orange
Yellow
Dark green
Bright green
Purple
Blue

Time for a **BRAIN 💡 BOOST** – in fact, you have worked so hard that you can have three.
Choose one oxygen boost, one happy brain boost and one fuel boost from pages 187–190.

Chapter 5

DIFFERENT INTELLIGENCES

Who's clever? ~ Different intelligences ~ What can you do about your intelligences and skills?

Who's clever?

Do you think you know who's clever in your class at school? Isn't it obvious? Isn't it the ones who do well in tests; the ones who can work out maths quickly; the ones who are great at reading, writing and spelling. Is that what you think?

When we look at these lucky or clever people, we assume they have better brains than others. We might even measure their cleverness with something called an IQ test. An IQ test is supposed to measure how clever someone is compared with other people. IQ tests have been used for more than 100 years, so they must be wonderful and accurate, mustn't they?

No. IQ tests measure only a certain type of intelligence. They measure how good you are at some number and word skills and particular types of logical thinking. Those things are important because they often show how well you will do at school, in exam-type subjects. But there's a lot more to being clever than that.

Imagine the following situation. I made it up, but things like this happen all the time.

Jennifer and Mark

Jennifer always does well in tests at school. She's good at most subjects, especially maths. All her teachers have noticed that she's clever. When she doesn't finish a piece of work or doesn't do brilliantly in a test, they say, 'Never mind – you must be tired,' and they give her help when she asks.

Jennifer's parents are proud of her, often boasting to their friends, and she wins three prizes when she leaves school. Everyone knows she'll get into a good university, and sure enough, she does. Easy. No effort needed – though of course, she works pretty hard. After all, everyone expects her to do well, so working hard is important to her. People praise her often so she wants to work hard. It's rewarding for her, makes her feel good. Being clever does make you feel good.

There's a boy in the same year, called Mark. Mark doesn't find schoolwork so easy. He doesn't come bottom in tests, but nearer the bottom than the top. He finds some subjects easier, but even if he tries his best he won't be near the top, not even in his best subjects. His teachers don't expect him to do well, but he doesn't behave too badly, so they mostly ignore him. If he doesn't finish a piece of work or does worse than usual in a test, teachers tell him off for being lazy. No one expects him to go to university, so no one suggests it; sure enough, he doesn't bother to apply. He doesn't see the point – after all, he'll probably fail anyway. He doesn't win prizes at prize-giving, but then no one expected him to, so that's ok, isn't it?

After university, Jennifer gets a job easily with a bank. For the rest of her working life, she earns a reasonable amount of money, and has no problems keeping a job. Every now and then she moves to work for another company or gets a promotion. She is quite happy with her life, though she wouldn't say she loves her work – it's just a job, and she does it just like most of the people she knows. You wouldn't say 'Wow! Jennifer's so clever!' She never becomes the boss or does anything very spectacular. Monday to Friday she works; evenings and weekends she does family stuff. She probably has a couple of children and maybe a dog. Or a cat. Well done, Jennifer – nice and steady, no worries.

Mark doesn't go to university, as I said. What I forgot to say is that Mark was in a band at school. The reason I forgot is that his teachers didn't think it was important. Well, it wasn't, was it? Not for school. Being in a band wasn't going to get him a job, was it? Besides, he played the guitar, so he couldn't be in the school orchestra, and as far as the music teachers were concerned if you weren't in the orchestra you were no musician.

Another thing no one ever noticed was that Mark was a great organizer – he organized his own music festival one weekend in his final year at school, and made some money. He was only sixteen. But the adults in his life didn't think that was very important either. After all, playing the guitar and organizing a gig were not signs of intelligence, were they? And it wouldn't get him a job. Would it?

But Mark was serious about this, more serious than anyone knew. Mark was the sort of person who could inspire others to do things; he made friends easily; he got things done. But that's not a sign of intelligence either, is it? Yes, his teachers and parents had noticed that he was always popular, always had crowds of pupils around him, but that wasn't intelligence, was it? In fact, they always said he spent too much time with his friends and his guitar, when he should have been working.

Soon after he left school at seventeen, Mark's band played a gig and he got the venue manager to agree to let him put on his own event the next month. Mark spent every waking moment organizing this; he made sure local newspapers and radio covered the story and he persuaded several minor celebrities to come. The event was a huge success and the venue manager was delighted. He gave Mark a job as his assistant. Over the next year, Mark learned everything he could about the business – and carried on playing in his band. After a year, Mark had saved enough money to think about renting his own venue for gigs. At this point, his parents started to realize that this was a boy who was going to go far, and they lent him the rest of the money he needed.

Jennifer, by the way, was still at university while Mark was doing this.

Within three years, Mark owned a successful nightclub, with radical new bands playing every weekend. He was earning good money, employing other people. He was a success, in business and in life. And he was still playing in his band for fun.

Within four years, he was earning more than Jennifer, had more freedom, and would have described himself as far happier. He buzzed with the joy of living.

As for his parents, how proud they were! Our son, the entrepreneur! Our son, the hotshot businessman! The big success, going places, his own boss! How clever he is!

Clever? But what happened to the boy who wasn't clever? The boy everyone ignored because he didn't shine at the things that schools and parents usually look for? The boy everyone wrote off as a loser?

Well, maybe Mark was clever after all – in things that schools don't always test or recognize. He was an organizer, an inspirer, a leader; he was musical and creative; he could talk to people, learn from them, yet be independent. Jennifer's strengths were mainly in maths and logic; she could learn what she was taught and repeat it in exams, and her language skills were good enough, so she could do well in most school subjects. But she wasn't clever in any of the things that brought Mark success in life and work.

Many of the world's most brilliant successes, even geniuses, have **NOT** seemed clever at school.

Most people now agree that there are many different ways to be intelligent. Some experts disagree that they should be called intelligences – perhaps we should call them 'ways to be successful'. They certainly are ways to be successful, but I don't think it matters very much what we call them in this book.

Different intelligences

We can't say exactly how many intelligences there are because it depends how you want to divide them. But experts on the subject talk about at least seven.[37] Let's take a look at them – then you can test yourself. And I bet you'll score highly in at least one of them. Maybe more than one. You could be brilliant, much more brilliant than you think!

Language ~ 'linguistic intelligence' – being clever with words and language. This is about reading, writing and talking. Of course, you could be good at reading but not writing, or good at reading and writing but not so good at talking persuasively and powerfully. Linguistic intelligence is very important at school and is one of the main things tested in IQ tests – though IQ tests don't test your talking or creative writing ability.

Logic/maths ~ 'logical/mathematical intelligence' – being clever with numbers and working out mathematical problems. Also very important at school – and it's the other main thing that IQ tests measure.

Looking ~ 'visual-spatial intelligence' – you need this for activities like reading maps, having a good sense of direction, working with graphs and diagrams and drawing. It's often not recognized at school, unless you do subjects like graphic design or craft, design and technology.

Music ~ 'musical intelligence' – not just your ability to learn musical instruments, but also things like musical memory (how quickly you learn a new tune, or how quickly you can recognize and name a tune you've heard before). It also enables you to identify what instruments or different musical elements appear in the piece of music you are listening to. Being able to tell whether something is 'out of tune' is also part of this.

Movement ~ 'kinaesthetic intelligence' – using your body, for sports, dancing etc. If you have good kinaesthetic intelligence you will find new sports easy. You will be good at aiming, throwing and catching. Hitting a ball with a racquet, judging distance, anticipating what your opponent is going to do, being able to learn sequences of movement for a dance – all these require good kinaesthetic intelligence.

Emotional intelligence[38] – not measured by normal IQ tests. This has two parts:

People skills ~ 'interpersonal intelligence' – getting on with other people. You might wonder what this has to do with intelligence, but some people find it harder than others: some people seem to know how to make and keep friends – others make mistakes over and over again. Teamwork and leadership skills also come into this, as well as the ability to understand other people's feelings.

Self-knowledge ~ 'intrapersonal intelligence' – knowing yourself, accepting yourself, knowing your strengths and weaknesses, and being able to change your behaviour when you need to, depending on the situation. People with this intelligence often do things like keeping a diary, or writing poetry.

Some people also talk about **'naturalistic intelligence'**[39] – being aware of and interested in nature and the natural world and how it works. Personally, I don't think this seems like a special intelligence, just an interest and a way of thinking, but I've included it because some people say it is an intelligence and it's quite interesting anyway.

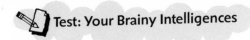 **Test: Your Brainy Intelligences**

Answer these questions as honestly as you can to find out where your intelligences are. Just put a tick, cross or question mark.

Linguistic

Do you know and use a lot of different words?

Do you find it quite easy to explain what you mean to people?

Do you like word games and puzzles, like crosswords or scrabble?

Do you enjoy reading?

Do you like to tell stories or write poems or make up the words for songs?

Do you enjoy listening to the words of songs?

When you write something, do you sometimes *get pleasure from* your words?

Logical/mathematical

Do you like maths and usually find new maths work quite easy to grasp?

Can you do sums in your head, without writing them down?

Do you like to know how and why things work?

Do you enjoy games like chess, backgammon, draughts, Sudoku?

Do you like experimenting, to see what would happen? (Including in science.)

Do you like putting things in lists, sorting into categories?

Do you like following instructions in order?

Body/kinaesthetic

Are you good at most sports that you try?

Do you enjoy working with your hands – for example, making things?

Are you good at subjects where you move around and stand up, such as drama?

Do you tend to be good at aiming and running?

Can you learn dance or other physical routines quite easily?

Do you have a good sense of balance?

Are sport, fitness and strength important to you personally?

Visual/spatial

Do you understand maps, charts and diagrams quite easily?

Can you do jigsaws easily and do you enjoy them?

Can you work out how things go together without instructions?

Are you observant? Do you sometimes notice things that others don't?

When you remember things, do you have a strong mental picture of them?

Can you describe a person you don't know well?

Are you good at drawing or design?

Musical

Can you learn tunes easily?

When you hear a tune that you've heard before, can you easily identify it?

Can you easily identify different instruments in a piece of music?

Do you learn facts more easily if you repeat them to a rhythm?

Do different pieces of music strongly affect your mood?

Do you tend to hum, whistle or tap when not listening to music?

Can you very easily tell when something is a tiny bit out of tune?

Interpersonal

Do you often guess what people are thinking or feeling?

Are you good at sorting out arguments?

Are you very interested in why people do things?

Do you like group situations – parties, clubs, team games, social activities?

Do you like giving advice to people and helping them?

Do you find it easy to organize people in a team so the task gets done and people work well together?

If someone is behaving badly, can you tell them without making it worse?

Intrapersonal

Are you an independent thinker, knowing what you want and like instead of always following others?

Do you have a hobby that you are quite happy to do on your own?

Can you quite quickly get over a strong emotion and move on?

If someone is mean to you, can you deal with it?

Do you have a good understanding of your weaknesses and strengths?

Are you ambitious? Do you want to work hard and shine at something?

Can you listen to sensible criticism and try to learn from it?

Naturalistic

Are you keen to know names of plants, flowers and birds and do you find it easy to see differences between types?

Can you learn and think better when you are outside rather than inside?

Would you prefer to have a view of hills and trees, rather than buildings and people?

When outside, do you often notice things that others miss, particularly sounds, smells, colours etc.

Do you or would you like to feed wild birds and/or other wild animals?

Do pollution, litter and environmental damage make you really angry?

If you are outside, do you notice and enjoy birdsong?

So, what are your strongest intelligences?

Did you discover that you have strengths that you didn't even know were important? Remember, each is very valuable. Some will help you succeed at school; others will help you more outside school. Different strengths are important for different jobs.

I have never met or heard of anyone who is brilliant at all of them, even people from long ago and people who are reckoned to have been geniuses. In fact, it would be very unusual to be brilliant at more than four or five, though you could be average at all or most of them.

Some other things you can be clever at

It seems to me there are lots of other skills – 'clevernesses', we might call them. They don't quite fit the intelligences mentioned above but are still useful to have.

Let's see what other skills you have. Be generous to yourself when scoring! If in doubt, give yourself a tick.

Planning and organizing ~ very important skills in so many areas of life. They can also help you to not be stressed if you are able to organize your work. Give yourself a tick if you are often able to:

- finish your work on time because you planned ahead;
- not be late for appointments;
- make lists so that you know what you must do (or keep a list in your head);
- say no to things that you don't have time for;
- plan your day or week so that you get everything done without panicking.

Controlling yourself ~ animals and very small children are less able to choose what to do, but as we get older we must learn to hold ourselves back and do the right thing even if it's not what we feel like. Tick if you are often able to:

- keep your temper – sometimes it's right to show that you are angry but losing control of your words or actions is not a good idea
- keep other emotions to yourself, when you want to – again, sometimes other people need to see your emotions, but being able to hide them can be useful
- keep a secret – when it's right to. (If a secret makes you uncomfortable, it's usually better to tell someone you trust.) Good secrets are secrets that involve a nice surprise for someone, or that stop someone being hurt.
- decide to save a pleasure for later – for example, you might decide to eat the chocolate after finishing your work; or you might decide to have

one piece now and another one later. You've seen
how bad my dog is at it;

- be tactful; say the right thing when someone is
  upset;

Leadership skills ~ this partly comes into interpersonal
intelligence, but it's a little more precise. Tick if you are
often able to:

- cope with the fact that some people may not
  agree with you;
- make decisions about what is best for a group or
  team;
- know how to work with other people and try to
  bring the best out of them;
- have good ideas about how to deal with a difficult
  situation – e.g. 'How will we persuade our head
  teacher to let us have a prom/disco/concert?' and
  work out a plan;
- persuade people to agree with what you suggest.

Remembering information ~ there are lots of types of
memory, and you are lucky if you can remember
facts easily. Tick if you are often able to:

- remember facts and names;
- remember the details of a story
- enjoy facts and figures, such as match scores and
  records;
- enjoy reading factual books because you want to
  know about real things;

- do quizzes involving knowledge (at least on topics that you like).

Seeking new experiences ~ wanting to learn new things means that you will open yourself to lots of new knowledge. The brain needs to be interested in what it learns – then it will find learning easier.

Tick if you:

- enjoy meeting new people;
- enjoy doing new things and learning new activities;
- get bored easily;
- go to look something up in a book, and then suddenly find yourself interested in something you weren't looking for;
- decide to try a new food in a restaurant, even though you're not sure you'll like it.

Creativity ~ you can show creative skills in all sorts of ways: painting, drawing, writing poetry/stories/plays, woodwork, sculpture, architecture, cookery, design.

Tick if you often:

- impress people with the things you create (in whichever of the above areas you are good at);
- have a real desire inside you to produce things of beauty or interest (music, art, writing etc.);
- have an idea/picture in your mind of what you are trying to create;
- want what you produce to be different, original, special;

✪ keep trying until you produce something that gives you real pleasure – though you may never be completely happy with what you've produced.

When you think about all the incredibly different skills we all need, you have to admire humans. And it's not surprising that lots of people who don't shine at school do very well in later life. Many of these skills and clevernesses can grow and change, and there's a lot we can do to have a better chance of being good at whatever we want to be good at – whether it's leading the country, discovering a new planet, writing a book, raising a happy family, teaching, nursing, building a house, working for a charity, or creating a beautiful garden.

What can you do about your intelligences and skills?

You can now:

- ✪ improve your strengths even more by practising them – remember, everything you do builds and strengthens connections in your brain;
- ✪ be proud of your strengths – they are signs of a good brain working well;
- ✪ work on areas of weakness – everything can improve, with practice;
- ✪ understand that although you can improve your weaknesses, your strengths will determine what sort of job you will enjoy most. People usually do what they enjoy because they usually enjoy what they are good at.

There's a saying: 'Knowledge is everything.' Well, no, it's not everything, but it is a huge start. When you know what's going on in your brain, that's when you can start to do something about it. You can take control of your brain and your life.

Time for a **BRAIN** 💡 **BOOST** – choose any two from pages 187–192

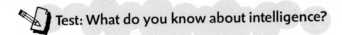 **Test: What do you know about intelligence?**

Before you answer these questions, look back at pages 100–102 and read over the paragraphs explaining each of the intelligences. Then look at the chart below and write the intelligence that you think is being used for each task.

Here are the intelligences, just to remind you:

Linguistic ~ Logical/mathematical ~ Visual–spatial ~ Musical ~ Kinaesthetic ~ Interpersonal ~ Intrapersonal ~ Naturalistic

TASK	WHICH INTELLIGENCE?
Reading a map	
Leading a team or group	
Learning a tune	
Dancing	
Doing a Sudoku puzzle	
Writing a poem	
Learning the names of different sorts of frogs	
Coping with someone saying something negative to you	
Knowing what someone else is feeling	
Playing a game of darts	

Chapter 6

DIFFERENT LEARNING STYLES

The three main learning styles ~ A fourth style ~ Some things to disagree about ~ What can you do with your learning style? ~ Are there other differences between the ways people learn? ~ Now that you know yourself, what now? ~ What about learning problems?

Long ago, school children sat in rows and listened to the teacher, who tried to teach them all in the same way. Only one learning style was allowed: the one the teacher thought best. If you were lucky, that suited you; if you were unlucky, you just had to try harder. You might have been very frustrated and felt stupid, even if you weren't. We now understand that different ways work better for different children – and teachers now look for ways to teach all children equally well.

If you can find what your learning style is, you could find learning much easier, and more enjoyable.

The three main learning styles

Visual ~ seeing and reading: visual learners learn better when things are displayed in pictures/maps, things they can look at. Visual learners rely on their eyes.

Auditory ~ hearing and speaking: auditory learners learn better when they can hear things read or said to them, and hear themselves say it too. Some auditory learners also learn well when music or rhythm is used to help memory. Auditory learners rely on their ears.

Kinaesthetic ~ learning through doing: kinaesthetic learners need to handle objects, do things with their hands, actually do something physical to help them learn. Kinaesthetic learners rely on their bodies, hands and feelings. They are sometimes called 'tactile' learners.

A fourth style

Reading/writing ~ preferring to use material that is written: these learners like lists, descriptions, written explanations, and would choose to trust and use written material rather than listen to someone telling them.

Sometimes this way of learning is not considered a separate style but it is such a strong factor for some people (me, for example) that I have included it.

Some things to disagree about

Not everyone agrees that we should take notice of different learning styles. They say that learning styles are just habits, and that they change as we grow older anyway, so we shouldn't focus too much on them. Maybe knowing what sort of learner we are might make us ignore our weaknesses, and they will get weaker. It can be very difficult for teachers to cope with all the different needs of a large class, as well – and what will the auditory learner be doing while the kinaesthetic learners are messing around with bricks or balance bars?

I understand all these arguments and some of them are good points. But I think that if you understand what helps you learn, you can learn more easily. And who wouldn't want that? Even if a teacher does not teach to our style, we can still use our own style for personal learning and revising.

Personally, I find that making diagrams and maps (for example Tony Buzan's well-known 'Mind-mapping') just doesn't work for me. But I know it's perfect for more visual learners. When people told me that Mind-mapping was brilliant and then I found I couldn't do it, I started to wonder what was wrong with me. If I'd been told that maybe my learning style was strongly of the reading/writing style, and not at all visual, I would have found things easier.

On the other hand, maybe someone should have helped me improve my visual skills so that Mind-mapping **DID** work! I'll never know.

I do know that discovering my learning styles has given me useful strategies. Because my brain is good with words and their sounds and meanings, I remember better if I attach delicious or vivid or weird words to the things I'm trying to remember. The kinaesthetic learner in me also needs the physical act of writing down things that I want to remember – seeing and hearing them is never enough. Mostly, though, I want descriptions, details, all written – I am useless at listening to stories read to me or radio programmes. I have always said I'm an information junkie – and it's true. I read information leaflets, brochures, documents over and over again, trying to get more meaning each time – and now that I know this is because of my learning style, I use written information even more and I organize it better too so that I can find it again when I want it.

It's all about knowing yourself. When you know yourself, you can work to improve the bits you'd like to improve, and value your abilities.

Test Your Learning Style

There are lots of tests like this. You may have done one at school. You can also find them on the internet. They are all very similar – just worded a bit differently depending on who they are for. I constructed this one myself, just for you, but it looks for the same information as the others. This one tests the three main styles, visual, auditory and knaesthetic.

Answer each question as honestly as you can. One learning style is **NOT** better than another. For each question, decide which one is the best for you. You will find some of the decisions quite hard and often you'll want to say yes to all three choices: just choose the answer that you **MOST** agree with.

---

1 If I need directions, I prefer to:

A use a map

B listen to someone explain to me

C follow my nose because I'll probably find it, and using a compass would be fun

---

2 When learning to use a new software program I'd rather:

A watch a teacher demonstrate first

B listen to someone explain first

C work it out as I go along

3 When learning facts for a test, it's better for me to:

A write lots of notes, with colours, and make lists and charts

B read my notes aloud or talk about them with friends

C make cards; act out stories/facts; walk about/go for a run while learning

4 When stressed about something, I usually:

A picture in my head what might happen

B have conversations in my head about it

C can't stay still, fidget, pace about

5 I would get most pleasure from:

A looking at some amazing pictures

B listening to music

C making something/doing something active

6 If I want to cook a new dish, I would:

A follow a recipe

B ask someone to explain first

C follow my instinct, tasting as I go

7 When I get a new gadget, I usually:

A read the instructions first

B ask someone who has had one before

C work it out by trying

8 The first thing I remember is:

A something I saw

B hearing something

C something I did or felt

9 If I had to learn the steps of a new dance quickly, I'd be better:

A writing/drawing the steps and going over them like that

B saying aloud the steps, talking them through

C doing them over and over again

10 When concentrating hard, I usually:

A focus my eyes on the paper/screen

B go over the things in my head

C fiddle, move things around, doodle

11 I'd prefer:

A to watch a film

B to listen to someone read an exciting story

C to learn a new skill

12 I think that when people lie:

A their eyes won't meet mine

B I can tell mostly by their voice

C I feel they're lying, but I can't explain why

13 When I meet someone new, I am most interested in:

A what they look like
B how they sound
C how they move about and stand

14 After meeting new people, I remember most easily:

A what they looked like
B their names
C what I felt like or did

15 If I had to explain something to someone, I'd:

A write down the instructions for them
B tell them how to do it, step by step
C show them first but then tell them to try it themselves

16 When clothes shopping, I mostly:

A imagine what something would look like on me
B ask someone what they think (friend or shop staff)
C try lots of things on

17 Listening to a band/orchestra, I am most interested in:

A watching the players/singers
B listening to the notes and words
C moving to the beat, feeling the music

18 I remember things best by:

A making notes and lists, sticking notes on my wall

B repeating them in my head or out loud

C doing things and imagining doing them

19 When I am angry, I am most likely to:

A keep picturing the thing or scene that made me so cross

B shout and tell friends how I feel

C throw things and stamp about

20 I more often say:

A 'I see!'

B 'I understand what you're saying!'

C 'I know how you feel!'

Your results:

Count how many **A**s, **B**s and **C**s.

You may find you are a complete mixture or you may find that you have many more answers in one column.

Mostly A – you are a visual learner.

Mostly B – you are an auditory learner.

Mostly C – you are a kinaesthetic learner.

Or do you think you are a reading/writing learner? Read these statements. The more statements you strongly agree with, the more likely that you are this sort of learner.

- Before going on holiday, I read as much as I can about the place I'm going to.
- When choosing a book, I always read a page first and don't only rely on the words on the back cover.
- A written description of a film would be better at persuading me to see it, rather than a poster or what my friends said about it.
- If I had an illness that I didn't know much about, I'd prefer to read about it on the internet rather than listen to the doctor explaining it.
- If I was designing a brochure to sell a product, I'd concentrate on what the words said, much more than the appearance and design.
- While choosing a course, I would read everything I could about lots of different courses – people telling me what they thought wouldn't be enough.
- If a teacher needed to give me feedback on my work, I'd rather have it written down so I could look at it closely.
- When I see a chart or diagram, I often don't know what to do with it at first – I would rather have the information written in words.
- I don't enjoy graphic novels because the pictures don't tell me enough.

- If a friend was reading and wanted to share something interesting, I would rather read it myself and not have the person read it to me.

What can you do with your learning style?

Look through the suggestions below. If your learning style came out as a mixture, pick any ideas that you feel would work for you. Even if you have one strong style, you still might find one of the other methods helps you. Be open-minded – see what works for you.

To make use of or develop a visual style

- Make pictures, maps, diagrams and charts when you need to learn things.
- Investigate Tony Buzan's 'Mind-mapping' methods
- Look for DVDs/videos of books that you are doing in school (though remember that the film is usually different from the book).
- Make pictures in your mind of the things you are trying to learn. If learning a sequence of events, imagine them like a film in your head.
- Use the internet and library to find pictures of the topics you are learning about – a librarian in a school or public library will help you.
- Use different colours when writing notes. Use arrows, underlining, exclamation marks and highlighters.
- When you picture something that you want to

remember, picture it in a silly and funny way. For example, if you want to remember how Henry VIII's six wives died, make a mental (or actual) picture of each of them with grossly exaggerated features – you can make them as rude as you like (as long as the wrong people don't see it, or at least you explain why you are doing it. But don't blame me...).

To make use of or develop an auditory style

- Speak aloud what you want to learn.
- Have a learning partner – test each other aloud or take turns in being the explainer.
- Record notes or facts onto a tape/CD (a digital voice recorder would be great, as you can transfer to a computer) and play them back.
- Make rhymes or rhythms to help you learn facts and figures; make a rap song; or pretend to drum to a beat while repeating whatever you are trying to learn.
- If you can't say things aloud (because you are in a test, for example) make a voice inside your head. Focus on the voice.
- Say the things you want to learn in a funny voice (make sure no one's listening...). Make silly rhymes – humour is a great memory aid.

To make use of or develop a kinaesthetic style

- Use cards and a filing box to keep your notes.

- Pin sections of your notes to walls and touch them as you learn them.
- Walk about while learning, especially outside.
- Allow yourself to move about as much as you want – even putting your body in a different position while trying to learn a fact can help.
- To remember the order of events (for example, in a story, or history topic, or a science experiment) write or draw each bit on a separate numbered piece of paper and lay them on the floor like stepping stones. Walk from one to the next while explaining that event.

To make use of or develop a reading/writing style

- Organize your notes and printed handouts in ring binder files or large notebooks.
- When you read something interesting, make a note of where you read it so you can find it again if you wish.
- Make use of lists and a diary to organize yourself and your work.
- Use your local library more.
- Many organizations will send you leaflets, free. Almost every organization has a website, so if you are doing a project or some research, you can usually find good written info, which they will send you.
- If you enjoyed a film, see if there's a book that the film was based on.

Are there other differences between the ways people learn?

Yes! Lots. These questions all tell you something else about your style of learning.

- Do you find it hard to stay still?
- Do you prefer or need silence when you work?
- Do you prefer background noise, like music?
- Do you prefer working alone or in pairs/teams?
- Do you feel very disappointed/upset when you don't succeed first time?
- Before you try a new skill, are you worried about failure?
- Do you need to be very sure of yourself before you start or are you happy to try and maybe fail first time?
- Do you ask for help quickly, or do you struggle on?
- If someone else is doing better than you, does that make you try less or more?
- If you can't do something right first time, do you keep trying till you get it?
- Do you work better in bright light or cosy dimness?
- Do you have more energy in the morning, afternoon or evening?
- If cooking a new recipe, would you rather an adult was with you to make sure you do it right, or would you rather be left alone?
- If following instructions, do you tend to follow them exactly?

- When you are doing something very easy, do you feel bored, or are you mostly happy that it's so easy?
- When the teacher starts to teach something new, do you feel happy and interested or worried and stressed?
- Do you prefer a classroom with everyone in rows or round tables in groups?
- If working in a group, are you more likely to be a leader or to wait for the others to have ideas?
- Do you like tests and check-ups to make sure you are doing OK?
- Do you prefer things with right and wrong answers, or discussions where people can disagree?
- Do you like working at a desk, sitting on a bed or lying on your stomach on the floor?

Now that you know yourself, what next?

You might want or be able to change some things; others you won't want or be able to change.

Decide which things you don't need to change. For example, preferring to cook a new recipe on your own is a perfectly good way of learning and won't cause any problems. You might get something wrong, but you'll learn from your mistake.

Although some things – like preferring to work alone – are perfectly OK, sometimes you won't have this choice. Being able to work in a team is useful, even if you don't like it. So, is there something you can do to make it feel better? For example, you might suggest that each person has a different job in the team; or you might simply do your best and be positive about it.

Finally, are some of your dislikes perhaps caused by having a negative view of yourself? Negative thoughts can stop you doing your best. For example, if failing once makes you not try again, you may miss out on being brilliant after some more practice. If you have a bad view of yourself, talk to someone – friends, parents, guidance teachers, anyone you trust. Everybody has some negative thoughts – no one is perfect. But there are ways to feel better about yourself.

And your brain will work better if it feels good about itself.

Can you change your school?

No, I don't mean can you go to another school! I mean, can you change the way your school is? If a group of you thought of a few changes that could make your classroom easier to learn in, your teachers might listen to you – if you said it cleverly. For example, perhaps your classroom would be easier to learn in if you could:

- arrange the desks differently;
- have an area for sitting on the floor;
- put flowers on a table, for everyone to look at;
- have a different colour on the walls;
- see different pictures on the wall;

❂ listen to background music sometimes

You never know what might happen if you ask. If it's something that will help you and your friends learn better, what teacher would want to ignore that? Talk to your parents too. They will also want to help you find the best way to learn.

What about learning problems?

As you know, everyone has different strengths and weaknesses. But some people have things they find *really* difficult, though they may be very strong in some of the intelligences described in Chapter 5.

You may have been told you have something with a name, such as dyslexia, dyspraxia, a speech disorder, or **ADHD** (attention deficit hyperactivity disorder). Or you may have sight or hearing problems.

If you have one of those conditions, there are lots of people to help you, and your school should be giving you special attention. If you feel you are not getting the help you need, ask your parents and teachers to help you more. You may think they know what's in your head but they don't. Not unless you tell them.

Other problems

Lots of people have things they find difficult but which don't have a special name. Perhaps you are:

❂ clumsy;
❂ very disorganized;

- poor at remembering things in order: e.g. instructions or routines;
- slow to write, even though what you write is fine;
- never able to finish a test or exam on time;
- someone who needs to hear things several times before you take it in;
- slow to understand what you read, even though you can read normally;
- a poor speller;
- someone who finds it very difficult to explain out loud, especially in front of an audience;
- very shy.

If any of these is a big problem for you, talk to any adult you trust. There are always strategies to help. There are tests to measure some of these things; and you might then qualify for extra time in public exams. For other difficulties, like being a poor speller, books and computer programs can help. If disorganization is your problem, making lists and charts and developing routines will be very helpful.

There's always a way. You may find that way yourself; or another person could give you a brilliant idea that you had never thought of. Talk!

TIP Check out the brain-polishing techniques in Chapter 7. They are good for everyone, including those with learning problems. Especially good is 'multisensory magic'.

Special brainy tips for brainy problems

Whether your difficulty is large or small, there are certain things that may help. Try whichever of these might work for you.

- Talk to the right teacher about all the things you find difficult. Make sure you are tested for anything that might be wrong.

- Have a homework partner. Doing homework with someone else is a good idea because you can each explain things to the other. BUT if you don't understand, don't be tempted to copy the answers – this will not help. Make a note that you did not understand and ask your teacher to explain.

- Record lessons (ask your teacher first) – this helps if you find it hard to concentrate on a voice, or if you are slow to make notes. Some teachers already record their lessons and allow pupils to download them from the school website. This is a brilliant idea.

- Carry a notebook and write down everything you are supposed to do – remembering instructions is difficult for some people (including me). I always think I will remember but I often don't if I don't write it down straightaway.

- TELL the teacher you have a problem and that you may need him or her to explain something again or to write it down.

- Try to combine your senses when revising – see 'multisensory magic' on page 143.

- Check your diet – are you eating all the right things and avoiding too much sugar and sweet drinks? Follow the food advice in Chapter 4.
- Don't give up on the things that are hard for you: find a way to beat them, slowly but surely. You may not always manage to turn a weakness into a strength but doing the best you can will always bring improvement – and pride. And remember – everyone has challenges to overcome.
- Look for websites that help. For example, the BBC has a whole section of learning sites for all ages, which will help you with homework, schoolwork and exams.

  www.bbc.co.uk/learning/subjects/schools.shtml

  And there are other websites listed on page 205.

Time for a triple **BRAIN BOOST** – have a protein snack, such as a ham and cheese sandwich; any of the happy boosts on page 189; and a non-sugary, non-fizzy drink.

Chapter 7

POLISHING YOUR BRAIN

Brain-training ~ Multisensory magic ~ Memory tricks ~
Whole brain ~ Extras ~ Brainy tips ~

Now you know a lot about how your brain works, and have already started to make it work much better. So you may be wondering what else you could possibly do that would make it even more brilliant. Well, I've found some extra tricks and ideas that could make your already amazing brain work like all the best designed machines: smoothly, easily, effectively and beautifully. I call it brain-polishing.

Brain-training

Brain-training involves a few simple but special daily exercises. It's nothing difficult or boring – in fact many of the activities are fun. And you only need to spend about five to ten minutes a day on it.

There are lots of books, gadgets and computer programs that you can use. Some of these also let you 'measure' your improvement. But you don't *need* to buy anything at all. Many of the exercises are things you can do yourself – though then it's harder to measure or record your improvement.

You might prefer to use a book or you might be a gadget freak – and by now you should be able to recognize your own preferences. But gadgets and computer programs often cost more than books, so you'll need to recognize that too.

To exercise your body you could spend a fortune on activities, gyms and expensive gear – or you could just go running or walking and kick a ball around with friends and spend nothing at all. It's the same with your brain – you do not have to be rich to have a super-fit brain.

What's special about brain-training exercises?

Now that you know that everything you do exercises your brain in some way, you may well ask, 'Why do I need *SPECIAL* exercises? Why can't I just do a whole load of different things, which will naturally improve all parts of my brain?'

Actually, you could. Some people who sell brain training items seem to think that only **THEIR** exercises are especially magical. I don't think it's that simple: I believe that doing lots of different things regularly is the best way to keep your brain in tiptop condition. **BUT** I also believe that the special brain-training exercises are good – it's just that they are not the only way. And they're not magic.

I've been doing several of the brain-training things that I mention below and some of the tests tell me that my brain has improved massively in a few weeks.

Could it be true? Sadly, I don't think so – the improvement is too huge. Is it just that I've got better at the things they are testing? Probably.

On the other hand, you know that everything you do changes your brain, and practising something makes certain parts of your brain stronger. So, if I exercise certain parts with special exercises, I could really be improving my brain, couldn't I?

Perhaps both things are true. Perhaps I have improved my brain a bit, but I have also got better at the things being tested.

People who recommend brain-training give scientific reasons. They say that, since different activities use different parts of the brain, if we find which activities use the greatest number of parts, then those will be the most effective ways to exercise the whole brain.

Brain-training aims to exercise as many parts of your brain as possible in five to ten minutes. And, if you think about it, it's not very practical to expect you to dance, nod to a rhythm, mentally add figures, read aloud, write, and work out a logic question all in the same few minutes. So, brain-training supporters say that it makes sense to find activities to do for a few seconds or minutes, which added together will exercise many important brain regions. Also we are more likely to keep practising something that is quick and easy, rather than something which will take hours and turn us into sweaty, exhausted wrecks.

A leading brain-training expert, Dr Ryuta Kawashima, explains that he has scanned people's brains while they do different things.[40] He says that, not surprisingly, while you are watching TV very few areas of your brain are active. More surprisingly, solving very difficult maths apparently uses only a tiny part of your brain.

Other findings include...

❷ Solving very easy maths very quickly uses lots of areas – and it's the speed that's important.

❷ Thinking about something very deeply, or meditating, uses a small area.

❷ Reading aloud uses more parts of your brain than reading silently – and reading aloud faster uses more than reading slowly.

❷ But even just reading silently uses quite a lot of your brain – much more than watching TV. This suggests that reading a book is using much more of your brain than watching a film of the book... Your parents are right!

❷ Writing also exercises a great deal of your brain.

Other brain-training theories focus more on improving a particular sort of memory called 'working memory'. Working memory only lasts for a couple of seconds and you use it to keep in your head the numbers you are supposed to be adding, or dialling on the phone, for example. Researchers in Sweden found that children who had brain-training for this sort of memory had higher IQ scores than those who didn't.[41] Improving this type of memory could really improve your brain in other ways.

What are the special activities?

If you do two or three of the following activities each day and try to vary them, you will be giving your brain a great workout. Some of them you'll need to find in a book or computer program; others you can just do yourself. I'll also give you a list of some books, computer programs, gadgets and websites.

Use a notebook to record what you did each day, and your speeds or scores.

- ✪ Fast adding of small numbers – to do this without a book or computer program, first write fifty pairs of single-digit numbers on a piece of paper, randomly, just any numbers at all. Then, get a clock with a second hand or use your computer clock, and see how quickly you can add each pair. See if you can get quicker over the week.
- ✪ Fast calculation – as above, except randomly adding, subtracting and multiplying.
- ✪ Read aloud for a couple of minutes a day.
- ✪ Speed read – get a passage of 300 words (if you use a computer you can use the word count facility) and read it aloud as fast as possible.
- ✪ Count aloud – how fast can you count from 1–120?
- ✪ Sudoku – good for short-term memory and

logical thinking; there are lots of books – start with easy puzzles and build up.

- ✪ Pelmanism/matching pairs – there are fun versions of this on websites or you can get a pack of cards: lay them face down; turn over two at a time; if they're the same number, leave them face up, otherwise turn both face down; how quickly can you find all the number pairs? Record your time. There's a fun (i.e. addictive) one at: **www.brainmetrix.com/memory/index**
- ✪ Word finder – how many words can you write down beginning with a particular letter, in one minute? Being able to find the words you want quickly helps speaking and writing.
- ✪ Word memory – get someone else to write down twenty-five words; look at them for ninety seconds, then cover them and see how many you can remember.
- ✪ Writing – write anything by hand. A daily diary?

Books, computer programs, gadgets and websites for brain-training

Here are just a few of the ones I've come across. I can't say which might suit you best but I've given them all a try and they all have their good points.

Brain Trainer ~ CD–ROM published by Mindscape: simple to use; gives a daily workout and records progress; contains fifteen different exercises for logic, number skills, word skills, memory, and spatial skills. You install it on your PC and do it every day, taking five minutes or so. Not expensive.

Brain Age ~ Nintendo DS game by Dr Kawashima: originally called Brain Training, it is a series of graded exercises to be done daily; good fun and very compelling. It claims to measure your 'brain age' – I'd like to believe it, because it very kindly gave me a brain age twenty years better/younger than my real age ... but I think it's meaningless. There's also a new extra game called Big Brain Academy. Apparently, doctors working with old people in Japan recommend this to keep their patients' brains active – any mental exercise is good for elderly brains.

Brain Trainer ~ electronic gadget by Flair: small, not very beautiful, hand-held device, much cheaper than Nintendo and doing less, but working on good principles; the exercises really do feel as though you are working your brain; records your scores on three different skills. Very useful for the price.

Train Your Brain ~ workout book by Dr Ryuta Kawashima, published by Kumon: daily exercises and assessments, including some interesting and challenging tasks. The Stroop Tests (also on the Nintendo version) are amazing – you have to look at the words 'red', 'blue', 'green', and 'yellow', all printed in different colours and name the colours, **NOT** read the words. So, if the word 'red' is printed in blue, you have to say 'blue'. Doing this at speed has the same effect on my brain as swimming five miles would have on my body. Exhausting. On the Nintendo version, you shout the answers at Dr Kawashima, which is quite satisfying.

Kids' 10-Minute Brain Workout ~ book by Gareth Moore, published by Michael O'Mara Books: exercises include typical brain-training tasks and many more. Great value and fun. There's an adult version to keep your parents' brains in shape!

Brain Metrix ~ website at **www.brainmetrix.com**: games and exercises for all ages, which will really test you. You can't keep your scores, so write them down if you want to chart your progress. Warning – there are a lot of adverts on this and other sites: do **NOT** respond without first checking with a responsible adult; some of the products advertised are expensive gimics and will exercise only your bank balance.

The Original Memory Gym ~ website at **www.memorise.org**: free exercises; good fun but, again, don't be tempted by the adverts. Remember: you do not have to buy anything at all to exercise your brain.

BrainConnection ~ there's a page on this website –

www.brainconnection.com/teasers – that has great exercises and games. I couldn't find any adverts, which made a pleasant change. A really interesting brainy site, with lots of info as well as games.

Multisensory magic

Good teachers know that pupils learn more easily if several senses are used at once. Teaching pupils with dyslexia always focuses on this, but it's something that can help all of us.

How do you do it? Think of the five senses: sight, hearing, smell, taste and touch. Let's look more closely at them and then I'll show you how you might combine them to help you learn.

Sight – including shape, colour and whatever you can do in your imagination to make something look interesting and noticeable. Words have shapes, and they can also have colours – if you write them in different colours. Use your visual imagination to paint strong pictures in your mind.

For example, I took ages to learn that messages between neurons go down the axon and into the dendrites of the next cell, not the other way round. So I imagined a tree standing on top of another tree and waving its branches in panic because of finding itself in an unusual (and scary) position. Suddenly I was able to picture the messages going down the trunk and into the dendrites (branches) of the tree below. Yes,

OK, it seems weird, but the point is that the vivid mental picture cured my confusion about which way messages pass between neurons. You can do this with anything you find hard to remember.

Hearing – hearing something said aloud (including saying it aloud yourself) helps fix it in your mind; and don't forget music and rhythm. Saying the things in a strange or silly or loud voice can help. Usually, there'll be some info you can remember well and others that you just can't seem to remember – use funny voices for the problem bits.

Taste and smell – these are closely linked to memory and using either when you are trying to learn something can really help. I have written this book while a particular scented candle has been burning – it won't make the book better but a) it has helped my mood and therefore made writing it even more of a pleasure than it would have been; and b) if I ever smell the same scent again I will powerfully remember writing the book. I will probably most strongly remember this particular sentence that I am writing now.

Touch and physical feeling – including the sense of movement. This is sometimes called the kinaesthetic sense, and is very useful for learning. Spelling is a skill that you can improve greatly by using this sense – for example, by practising writing a word over and over, to fix in your memory the feeling of writing it.

How to combine your senses to make Multisensory Magic: Learning spellings

Even good spellers have sticky words that they find hard to remember. You will know what your sticky words are – probably words that don't fit rules, or two words that sound the same but have different spellings. Here are some multisensory methods.

- Get a long narrow piece of paper and copy the word correctly at the top. Look closely at the word, and say the letters aloud, writing them as you say them (in your usual handwriting). Now, trace over them several times, saying the letters as you write them. Then, fold the top of the paper over so you can't see it, and try to write the word below, saying the letters aloud again. Check you've done it right. Do this fifteen times, checking each time. Now do it with your eyes shut, so that you focus on the movement.
- If one part of a word always causes you a problem, do the same as above, but *SHOUT* the problem letters and press harder with your pen. Or say those letters in a funny way and write them bigger.
- If you have trouble with words that do fit patterns, take one set of words (for example the ones with 'ei' – like weird, receive, deceive, receipt, beige) and write them all in the colour beige (light brown)

on one piece of paper, while saying the words aloud; decorate with as many beige-coloured things as possible; if you use a computer, it's even easier.

Then, write words which have 'ie' (e.g. niece, field, friend, belief, believe, brief, chief) in white on a black background; decorate with white things. You can work out how to deal with any group of words in this way. (Yes, I know there's a rule about ie/ei, and you can learn that too, but it's just one way of doing it. And the rule has exceptions, like all rules.)

Learning what happened in what order –

This is useful in history, for example, or when remembering anything else that has to be in order. I use this method when I'm learning the sequence of a talk or lecture.

⊗ Write/print out each section in a different colour. For me, the order is always red, blue, green, black, red, blue, green, black etc. so if I practise the talk with my notes in those colours, I can remember the order I want to say things. For example, it will be fixed in my head that a certain point was red and another was blue, so when I've said the red one, I'll know the blue one is next. It helps if there's something about the first and fifth points that makes me think of red – but for me the letter A always feels red, so I try to make that point begin with A or have a heading beginning with A.

- Also, read the parts aloud. You could read each part in a different voice (I haven't tried this but maybe I will next time). I could have my red voice, blue voice, green voice etc. Your red voice could be angry, your blue voice could be sad, your green voice could sound as though you feel sick.

- Bring smell and taste into it by imagining, for example, a cut-up lemon while visualizing the story; imagine taste, smell and colour. If your mouth hasn't started to produce saliva, you didn't imagine it properly!

Learning facts and figures

- Give your facts or figures a rhythm; make a rap or a song.

- Use smell: while learning for a test, sniff a favourite smell: for example, vanilla, perfume, soap, coffee, lemon oil. Then, when you have the test at school, take that smell on a tissue and smell it while doing the test. Don't choose a smell that all your friends find revolting. Mind you, it could be a way to put them off *their* tests...

Memory tricks

There are so many ways to polish your memory that people have written whole books about the subject. Here are some of the most popular.

- **Mnemonic sentences** – 'mnemonics' are anything that

help your memory, and the first m is silent, in case you are trying to get your tongue round that. To learn a list of things, take the first letter of each and make a sentence to remind you of the order. When I was at school I learned all the British prime ministers from 1852 to 1918 using that method – I am not telling you what the rather long sentence was (because you'd think I was mad) but I can still remember them. Yes, OK, it's not fantastically useful because no one ever asks me to tell them, but you never know.

- ✪ **Rhyming numbers** – this is for remembering numbers in order, for example the numbers of a password. Imagine that each of the numbers 0–9 has a rhyming picture associated with it. The ones many people use are: 0 – hero, 1 – gun, 2 – shoe, 3 – tree, 4 – door, 5 – hive, 6 – sticks, 7 – heaven, 8 – gate, 9 – wine. Once you've learned those, you can use them often. For example, if you wanted to remember the number 6802305, you could imagine a huge pile of *STICKS*, in front of a locked **GATE**; you need to find a HERO, so you throw your *shoe* high into an apple *tree*, and a HERO falls out of it and lands on a bee **HIVE**. No, it's not a story that's going to win any prizes, but if you picture the parts vividly you should remember the numbers.
- ✪ **Sausage links** – similar but not about numbers. Imagine you have to learn a list of words, either in a particular order or not. If you link each one to

the next by making a story (as for the rhyming numbers above) you'll remember them more easily.

✱ *Loci* – this latin word means 'places', but it's a method the ancient Greeks used too. There are different methods but here's one: picture a building that's very familiar to you (such as your house or school). First work out a journey through the building, in a sensible order, picturing each room as you do. After you've done this once, you keep the same journey for every time you use this memory trick. Take the first piece of info that you are trying to learn and associate it strongly with the first room – supposing you have to remember that the story of *Macbeth* starts with the three witches: imagine the witches in your first room, all smelly and crusty with straggly hair, sitting in your sofa; then picture the characters of the next scene in the next room of your house. Take each stage separately and fix it in your mind before going to the next one. Make your mental picture as strong as possible.

There are lots of books that explain memory tricks in much more detail. Try *Brilliant Memory* by Tony Buzan.

Whole brain

You know this now: the best way to keep your brain in tiptop working condition, ready for all the new things you'll learn in later life, is to exercise all parts of it. So, include activities in all of these areas:

- ❁ Logic and maths – Sudoku is a brilliant, fun exercise. You can find books of Sudoku puzzles for all ages.

- ❁ Language – you probably do lots of this at school, but don't forget to read for your own pleasure too; and talk a lot, to friends, to adults, to your dog... Read aloud – it uses different parts of your brain and requires more concentration than silent reading.

- ❁ Music – listen, and take part if you can; even tap the beat in your own room if you aren't a performer.

- ❁ Visual/spatial – use your eyes, use maps, draw diagrams even if you don't like to, draw pictures even if you don't show anyone. I used to be quite good at drawing, but now I am ashamed of my pictures because I've stopped practising and I feel useless – as part of brain-training, I am trying to draw something every day.

- ❁ Kinaesthetic/body – practise aiming and throwing – throwing things in the bin is a good idea. Improve your balance – stand on one leg with your eyes shut. Try juggling.

- ❁ Interpersonal – think about someone you don't know well and imagine what she/he is feeling. Next weekend, persuade all your friends to do something you've never done before, and organize the whole thing.

- ❁ Intrapersonal – you're doing **A LOT** of that in this book. You don't need to do any more!

If you do all those things, your brain will be beautifully well exercised all over.

Extras

Chewing gum? Several studies have shown that chewing gum might help concentration and therefore learning and memory. A study in 2002 showed that it increased heart rate, making more oxygen flow to the brain. But be careful – very large amounts of chewing gum are not recommended. Choose sugar-free and just a few pieces a day. Whatever you do, dispose of it properly: chewing gum on the floor is something that raises my heart rate to positively dangerous levels.

Talk to yourself – if your concentration wanders, speak sternly to yourself, saying, '**STOP**! Stay here!' I'm not joking – many people recommend it.

Neurobics – do the opposite of what you normally do. Do your teeth with the wrong hand; write with your eyes shut; read something upside down. Doing something unusual keeps you alert and exercises your brain.

The Mozart effect – research shows that listening to some types of music can help concentration.[42] Mozart has been singled out as the musical magician. Even rats learned their way round a maze more quickly after listening to Mozart than other music. BUT, take note: in later studies, the same effect was not always found; also, any effect may be because the music makes us feel happy or relaxed. There's no real evidence that listening to Mozart improves your 'intelligence' – but if it helps your concentration you may find your brain takes in information more easily. Some companies have produced expensive products for young children and babies, but they are not necessary: all you need do is listen and enjoy.

On the other hand, lots of research shows that learning to play an instrument does help other learning abilities, particularly in maths. Just listening isn't enough – you actually have to play. Some research showed that learning to play an instrument improved memory for words.[43]

It's also well-known that different sorts of music have different effects on mood. Something familiar and soothing is a better background while you're working than something clashing and stressful. If it distracts you, turn it off. You shouldn't be **THINKING** about the music if you are trying to work.

Play your cards right – playing card games is great for memory, logic, strategy and enjoyment.

Chunking – most people learn best if they only have a small number of new facts at once. This is called chunking. Most people find the best number of chunks is four. So, learn four spellings, numbers, dates or names at once. Don't move on till those are learnt.

Focus – don't try to do too many things at once. We can't focus on one thing very well if we are trying to focus on other things. So, don't allow yourself to be interrupted: tell people you are working so you won't be disturbed; switch email off; switch your mobile off; finish one task before starting another.

Repeat; repeat; repeat – to fix something in your memory, repeat an hour later, then the next day, the next day, the next week, the next month.

Early birds – it's said that brains work better in the morning than at other times. Some people feel groggy first thing though, but once you've woken up and had something good to eat, your brain should be most alert in the morning. However, lots of other things will affect you and personally I work better in the late afternoon, mainly because by then I am starting to panic about how much I've got to do and a little bit of panic (not too much) kicks my brain into action. As long as my brain and body are properly nourished with food, water and oxygen, I can rely on working really well at this time of day. Find what works for you and use it.

Run for it – in one study, rats that ran a lot increased the number of new neurons in the hippocampus (important for memory) and double the number of new cells survived, compared with rats that didn't run much. Maybe running will do the same for us. I'll leave it to you to find out because I'm quite happy with all my other exercise and brain-training. And I walk the dog a lot.

Bend over backwards – in yoga, stretching and bending are believed to affect the mood and the brain in different ways. Bending backwards may improve your mood best of all. But not if you hurt your back, so go easy...

Become a nun – a bit extreme, perhaps, but you might like to know about research into 678 nuns in Minnesota.[44] These nuns were aged between 75 and 107 and were remarkably healthy, with brains that seemed in wonderful working order. And when 104-year-old Sister Matthia died and was examined, her brain was found to have no signs of excessive aging. The research suggested that the reasons included: positive emotions, mental activities such as crosswords, physical activities such as knitting and exercise, and plenty of folic acid in the diet.

On the other hand, being a nun is quite a sheltered life and perhaps less stressful than many others, so maybe it's their lack of stress that's important. And one of the nuns apparently mentioned a big disadvantage to being a nun: 'Think no evil, do no evil, hear no evil, and you will never write a best-selling novel.'

Odd personal habits – I am not actually recommending these, but I thought you might like to know that, *apparently*:

- Edgar Allan Poe worked with a cat sitting on his shoulder;
- Victor Hugo wrote with no clothes on;
- C. S. Lewis wrote standing up;
- Voltaire used his lover's naked back as his desk.

They were all authors. I, on the other hand, am completely sensible. Except that when I'm writing, I have a candle burning on my desk, even in the middle of a sunny day. And I talk to the dog. When she starts to talk back, that's when I'll begin to worry.

Brainy tips

There's so much to remember in this book that I thought I'd remind you of some brainy tips. Next to each item, there's a page reference so you can find the details if you want to.

- **Care for your brain** – with good food, water and oxygen. Make sure you have food and drink before working. p.55

- **Know your learning style** – and work with it. p.119

- **Value your own intelligence** – there are many ways to success. p.95 onwards

- **Exercise all parts of your brain** – use numbers, words, music, the senses and physical activity. p.149

- **Try new things** – keep your brain alert. p.88

- **Be kind to yourself** – your brain works better when it's happy. p.83

- **Control your environment** – create a comfortable place where you can work well. p.87

- **Organize yourself** – split work into chunks and make lists of what you have to do. p.127 or 106

- **Use memory and learning tips** – find ones that work for you, and practise them. p. 139

- **In short, know your brain** – feed it, test it, stretch it.

 **Test: How Polished is your Brain?**

Time to test just how shiny it is!

Test 1
Read these words and study them for two minutes.

Use multisensory methods to try to remember them: say the words aloud as well as looking at them. Picture each one as vividly as you can. Try to imagine it in as great detail as possible. If there's a word you can't picture because it isn't an object, find another way to imagine it – for example, if there was the word 'laugh' you could imagine a person laughing really annoyingly. You can write them if you want to, but you haven't got much time.

candle	salt	heaven	hope	music
tree	cake	silly	hop	paper
baby	house	fat	plate	thistle
match	catch	hat	parcel	chicken

Now cover the list and see how many you can write down from memory.

How many did you get?

16–20 – memory genius

11–15 – excellent

5–10 – pretty good

0–4 – hmm, bit of memory training needed!

If you didn't do as well as you would have liked, maybe there was a reason – hungry? Thirsty? Tired? Done too much today? Someone annoying you? All sorts of things can spoil your concentration.

Test 2

Here's another list of words and you've got two and a half minutes but this time use a different memory trick: sausage links. Make them into a story, linking them together.

star	fear	tree	and	music
tree	sandstorm	horse	fairy	tramp
bottle	rain	fat	boy	whistle
cut	mountain	castle	fish	pink

Test 3 – mental maths

You'll need a timer because you have to do these sums as fast as possible and record how long it takes you.

$3 \times 4 =$ $13 - 3 =$

$2 + 6 =$ $6 - 1 =$

$1 + 7 =$ $9 + 2 =$

$9 + 3 =$ $9 \times 1 =$

$8 - 8 =$ $9 - 8 =$

$3 + 8 =$ $17 - 3 =$

$8 - 7 =$ $2 \times 9 =$

$1 \times 7 =$ $7 \times 1 =$

How long did you take? Less than 25 seconds? BRILLIANT!! But whatever you scored, the important thing is to try to make that score better by practising like that each day.

Test 4 — Logic

If you enjoy Sudoku puzzles, you could buy a book of them (start with simple ones for your age group). I didn't enjoy Sudoku at first but now I am well and truly addicted. And of course, my brain just gets better...

Each row needs to have each of the numbers 1–6. Each rectangle of six squares and each row can only have a particular number once.

	2	4	3	6	
5					1
4		2	5		6
6		3	2		4
2					3
	4	1	6	5	

Here's another for you to try.

		5	3		
	1	6	2	4	
5	6			2	1
1	2			6	3
	5	2	1	3	
		1	6		

Test 5 — Wordy stuff

How quickly can you match these bits of word to make whole words? Each whole word is made of two bits.

bat	pie	ad	ce	dle	rot
can	pre	kle	car	pre	place
ern	sal	cream	sill	patt	mag
tic	ice	tle	ce	fire	ry
pare	cel	net	let	sand	pig
wich	pea	tty	par	y	cur

Something to think about

Remember what I said at the beginning – that your brain is everything that makes you you? Well, your brain is now different from when you started to read this book. You have changed your brain. Literally. It is physically different from how it was before you read this book. You have changed you. You have grown new connections and made your brain better able to learn and be the best it can be. That's amazing! And it's only the beginning: now it's up to you to keep looking after your brain, making it as good and healthy and happy as it can possibly be.

Enjoy it!

Chapter 8

FUTURE BRAINS

For better or worse? ~ Neurofeedback ~ Brain-changing drugs? ~ Brain-changing food? ~ Mind-reading and thought control ~ Messing around with genes ~ Brain implants ~ Your future brain

For better or worse?

One thing's certain – this is not the end of the story. Scientists are learning more about the brain all the time. They are also looking at ways to change it – to cure diseases, repair damage, and to give our brains extra power. The future holds amazing new possibilities.

This chapter is about some things that scientists are working on now. Some have already begun to be reality; others are on the way; some may be far in the future; others may never work. Do we want all of them? How much do we want to mess around with our minds and brains? Might we cause different problems by mistake? You'll discover some of my opinions during this chapter – and maybe you'll have some opinions that are different. That's the whole point – we have to think about things and discuss them.

163

Of course, we want to be able to cure people of brain illnesses or problems that make their lives painful or short. Making damaged brains work properly is one of the excellent aims of neuroscientists. But that's not all we have to think about.

What about trying to make healthy, 'normal' brains even better? We'd all like to be able to do more, wouldn't we? To have better memories, which can understand more, add faster, think better? If it's OK to choose good food to make our brains work better, why not take a pill for the same reason? Or have something implanted in our brains to improve some skills?

By the way, what do we mean by a 'normal' brain? We could have a long discussion about that! Of course, sometimes it's hard to say whether one brain is 'normal' or not. For this book, I mean a brain that is not ill or damaged, a brain that works as well as most brains do – maybe not perfectly, but reasonably. Some normal brains will be better at some things than other normal brains. The owners of some normal brains might think they have a bad memory (like me) or a poor musical ability (me again) or can't do maths (help!), but they would still not consider their brains damaged or abnormal.

We can improve our normal brains, of course, which is what this book has been about, but the idea of improving normal brains raises tricky questions. We are going to have to think carefully about these things now and in the future, as you will see.

If people decide to use medical or scientific treatments to make their healthy brains even better, here are some things to think about.

- **What about side effects?** Any medical treatment can have side effects and these can be damaging or unpleasant. Sometimes we don't know the side effects till too late. If someone is ill, they might risk it but would you want to risk damage if you are healthy?

- **What about those who can't afford the treatment?** Do we want to make life even harder for people who already struggle to make ends meet?

- **Perhaps our brains need to be as they are** – making them better might have unwanted results. For example, perhaps our memories are designed to forget much of what we learn, and if we remembered everything perhaps we could not cope. Evolution – the natural process which takes thousands of years – has given us brains and bodies fit for success: if we disturb that, might there be a bad effect that we didn't predict?

- **Unfair advantages?** Would it be like athletes using drugs? Of course, some people have advantages anyway – being born with better brains or special talents or having a better education or a happier childhood or more opportunities – so perhaps taking a drug would be no worse than that? Is it fine for one person to have a brilliant brain through good luck, but wrong for someone else to make his or her brain brilliant with a medical treatment?

What do I think?

I think there are lots of things we can and should do to improve our brains. But I am against taking any pill or drug to improve my brain, unless I'm ill. How can I possibly argue that? How can I say, 'Yes, eat plenty of oily fish and yogurt because they have chemicals that will help your brain work, but no, don't take a simple pill with chemicals that seem to do exactly that'? Because I'm a boring adult? No. Well, I may be, but it's not why.

Very simply, as far as we know, eating a reasonable amount of fish/soya/yogurt (or any of the other foods recommended in Chapter 4) every day will do our brains lots of good and no harm at all; but we do *not* know that taking any drug or other medical treatment will do a healthy person lots of good and no harm at all. In fact there are lots of reasons to suggest that it might do you some harm. And it is my strong belief that we have each been given one brain and that it is our duty to look after it, keep it safe, and make it the best it can be without taking bad risks with it. And taking a drug or having a medical treatment when you are not ill is, I believe, a very bad risk.

I believe that there could be many bad results from people taking steps to use machines or drugs to improve an already healthy and normal brain: unwelcome effects on people's health and happiness and on the general working of our society. I see a difference between doing the things in this book that can help your brain grow 'naturally', without any possibility of overdoing it or harming it, and doing something medical or mechanical to make a sudden and dramatic change to the way a brain naturally works.

But you are very welcome to disagree with me! Just use your brain while you're doing it. In other words, *think* – a brilliant way to improve your brain naturally.

Some special things to think about

Techniques will come along which might have great benefits for curing serious brain illnesses or damage, but which we might think were wrong.

Supposing I had a brain tumour but scientists could remove that brain section and replace it with a transplanted part of someone else's brain, someone who had just died? On the one hand, it could save my life; on the other hand, if the brain is where our personalities are, wouldn't I then have part of that other person's personality or memory? We are nowhere near being able to do this, but we may have to think about it one day.

Supposing a machine was invented that could read your thoughts? This would be useful for detecting whether a suspect was lying about a crime, wouldn't it? But what if the technology was used secretly – for example, when you were talking to your doctor, your boss, your teachers or your parents? Scientists are working on this now – the army would love to have mind-reading technology and governments will fund it for that reason.

Or what if a machine could not only read your thoughts, but change them? What a brilliant way to defeat your enemies – change their thoughts so that they agree with you and stop fighting you. Yes, brilliant until someone does it to you...

Just because we can do something, it doesn't mean it is a good idea. On the other hand, once something can be done, it usually is – even if there are laws against it.

Decisions like this are nothing new – often in the past we have had huge debates about whether a new medical advance is good or bad. Before the nineteenth century, many thought it was wrong to cut up a dead human body; in earlier times, people thought it was pointless anyway because humans were nothing like other animals; people have believed that it was wrong to give women anything to help their pain in childbirth because they thought this pain was 'God's will'. When Louise Brown, the first 'test-tube' baby, was born in 1978, many people thought it was wrong to 'mess around with nature' by fertilizing a baby in a test tube. Since then, more than a million test-tube babies have been born around the world and now most people agree it's a wonderful treatment for many couples who can't have babies without this help.

And there are many things today that people disagree about. Here are some examples.

- ✪ Is it right to use special cells called **stem cells**, taken from unborn babies, to cure serious illnesses? These cells come from the tissue of **embryos** that have not survived to birth.

- ✪ Is it right to screen unborn babies at a very early stage to select one that does not have certain problems – and therefore 'de-select' (i.e. terminate) those who have a defect? And what is a 'defect'? A serious illness such as Huntingdon's disease, or short-sightedness? Supposing you were expecting a baby and you were told you could choose between an embryo that had the gene for short-sightedness and one that seemed 'perfect' – which would you choose? Well, I'm short-sighted, so what does that mean for me?

- ✪ Or what about **cloning** animals – and perhaps one day humans? Even if it is illegal, someone, somewhere is probably trying to do this.

We can't stop science. Anyway, science has given us huge benefits, cures for diseases that we'd have died of hundreds of years ago and machines that make our lives comfortable and exciting in ways that our ancestors could only dream of. So we don't want to stop science. But we need to know what's going on, because that's the only way we can be part of the arguments.

Let's look at what scientists are doing now.

Neurofeedback

Neurofeedback is already with us. I put it in this chapter for two reasons. First, it's not something you can do yourself or easily buy – yet. Second, it's very new and changing all the time. In the future, neurofeedback will probably be something you can do at home. It might even be a part of your school day. When my parents were young, children had to have a daily dose of cod-liver oil; when some of you have your own children, it could be a daily ten minutes of neurofeedback.

What is it? It's thought control – but you control it. The idea is that if you are hooked to a machine that measures your brainwaves, you can change them simply by ... well, no one can explain what to do; you just do it by trying.

Imagine looking at a computer screen and being able to move an object on it just by thinking about it. Well, that's what happens in neurofeedback. What you see on the screen is linked to your brainwaves, and you are given a task. For example, 'Make that car move faster.' You concentrate hard and soon discover what to do with your thoughts to make the car move faster. And this alters your brainwaves and helps your particular problem.

Another way is to use a scanner to show what part of the brain is lighting up. Suppose you are suffering a lot of pain – the doctor shows you the pain centres of your brain lighting up and tells you to try to calm that activity. For some amazing reason, you find you can. And the pain disappears.

Neurofeedback has also been successful for treating stress, anxiety, depression, epilepsy, **strokes**, tinnitus and paralysis. There are reports that it has brought people out of comas.

This all sounds wonderful. But it's expensive. That means that there's money to be made: we must make sure that the people offering it are properly trained and that customers are not conned. I am sure that one day, perhaps soon, people will be able to use this easily at home. It certainly offers a great deal of hope for people with injuries and illnesses. But there may be risks or reasons to be careful.

Of course, as with all the other scientific discoveries, even people who are healthy will probably want to use it. As you already know, there could be problems with that.

Brain-changing drugs?

Imagine taking a pill to make you more intelligent. Or to make you more awake and better able to concentrate. Well, forget imagining it – it's already here. All these drugs were invented to help people with illnesses but healthy people might want them too. Would you be tempted?

- You may have heard of Ritalin. It's often given to children with ADHD (attention deficit hyperactivity disorder) to help them learn and concentrate better. It is also sometimes used by people who **DON'T** have ADHD, to help them concentrate.

- Many scientists are working on drugs to fight **Alzheimer's disease** – (a disorder that destroys parts of the brain). This would be wonderful, I am sure you would agree. The same pills could also improve normal brains.

- You probably haven't heard of **ampakines**.[45] These drugs are being tested now. They aim to help all sorts of brain disorders and improve memory in people with brain problems; but they could improve the memories of other people too. A study in the UK showed that this was the case.[46]

- Pills instead of sleep? Soldiers and pilots sometimes take drugs to keep them awake for long periods of time – and you can see why they might need them. Scientists are working on better versions to help keep us awake for longer. This might be useful for some other jobs, too, and it might be very tempting for anyone – you'd have more time to have fun, and more energy for everything. But can our bodies cope? What damage might we be doing by avoiding sleep?

- Drugs to control mood? There are already drugs

that make you less angry, less sad, less emotional, less hyper, less lazy, less nervous, less frightened, less stressed. Scientists are looking at more and better ways to do this. And for people who are seriously ill, such medicines prescribed by a good doctor can be really helpful. But what about people who are not ill, but who just fancy not feeling sad, or angry, or emotional? Perhaps we should accept that we cannot always feel 100 per cent happy or calm. Perhaps it is better for us to find other ways to deal with things we don't like. Do we want to drift through every up and down of life controlling all our feelings with pills?

Brain-changing food?

You already know about foods that are good for your brain. But scientists are trying to identify which chemicals in those foods help us, so that food manufacturers can add them to other foods.

- They are investigating adding substances such as choline, brahmi, gingko biloba, ginseng, cocoa, fish oil, and folic acid. So, burgers that make you brilliant? Clever chips? Brainy bread? Memory milk? Mathematical macaroni? Logical lollies? Smart sweets?

Well, that would be good, wouldn't it? But would it? Should manufacturers and governments control what we eat? Why can't we just eat good food in its natural state? Why can't we make healthy choices ourselves?

Also, if these nutrients are added, isn't there a risk that some of us might consume too much of something? Babies and young children might be damaged by high doses of substances. Just because something is 'natural' doesn't mean we can stuff ourselves with it. For example, choline is dangerous in very high doses.

On the other hand, it's easy for well educated people to make the right choices and understand complicated messages about healthy food – and shouldn't we protect less lucky people by making sure they have the right vitamins? So, perhaps governments *should* ask manufacturers to put brain-improving chemicals in our bread (as they used to do with vitamins during the Second World War). What do you think?

What about extra high vitamin doses?

There's evidence that vitamin supplements can improve the concentration, behaviour and IQ of people who have had a poor diet. This is not new – as far back as the Second World War, people noticed that children who were given extra vitamin C and D seemed to behave better. A new study in the UK is going to offer vitamin supplements to some convicted criminals to see if it improves behaviour, as has been shown in several US studies.[47]

Hang on a minute! Didn't I say on page 63 that you

don't need vitamin supplements because you should get everything you need from your food? Yes, I did, because that's what diet experts say and what I believe. Just because vitamins are good for your brain doesn't mean that the more you take the cleverer you will be. Very high doses of some ordinary vitamins, such as A, D and E, can have unpleasant side effects. In fact, on the very day that I am writing this, a report has been published that shows that high doses of some common vitamins give a greater risk of early death.[48] And this is nothing new either – other studies have come to the same conclusion over the last few years.

The clear message is: you should have enough vitamins but not overdo it with high-dose supplements.

Mind-reading and thought control

A machine that reads your mind and then changes your thoughts? In the past, only science fiction writers thought much about this. In the future, it may become reality. In fact, in some ways it has already.

A thought is simply some neurons being activated. If scientists can see which groups of neurons are activated when you are attached to a machine or scanner, they can tell something about what you are thinking. Let's look at some of the things they are working on.

- **Transcranial magnetic stimulation** – this sends magnetic pulses through wires placed on the head. It can switch particular thoughts on and off and it is already used to treat depression, pain and schizophrenia. Imagine if this got into the wrong hands and your thoughts could be interfered with.

- **Lie detectors** – police and the courts would love to have a machine that would show who was telling the truth. At the moment, these are not reliable – but they are improving.

- **The god spot** – there are areas in the brain that are active when someone is having a religious experience. The idea of a 'god spot' in the brain began in 1997 when researchers found that if they activated an area with a small electric current, people felt they were having a religious vision.[49] (Since then other studies have shown several areas, not just the one god spot). In the experiment, they were volunteers, but what if scientists found a way to interfere with your thoughts without you knowing? What if a religious group wanted its members to be more strongly religious so they activated people's god spots as they arrived at church/mosque/synagogue/temple?

- **Are you a racist?** Scientists[50] claim to be able to watch your brain and detect racist tendencies even if you try to hide them. Could employers use this one day? And perhaps not just for racism but beliefs that your employer simply did not like. And what if you know your thoughts are bad or wrong, and you act properly in every way, but can't change the way you think? Ah, well – maybe you'd sign up for 'thought control', to have your views changed. Maybe you'd be forced to.

- **What are you going to do?** Scientists are working on predicting what someone plans to do. You might think this would be useful as security, to detect people planning terrorist activity, for example, but how reliable would it be? And if you arrested someone, how would you **PROVE** they planned to commit a crime? And what if someone had a bad thought that crossed their mind, almost like a piece of imagination or a fear, and the machine decided that this was actually what they were planning to do? Imagine you were a novelist planning a really gruesome, gory and shocking book – would *these* thoughts show up on the scan? Some very nice people write some very nasty books...

- **Will you be a murderer when you grow up?** Some scientists believe that the brains of killers often look different. If they get the technology right, should we all be screened to make sure we don't have the brain of a killer? What if we find someone with the brain of a killer – do we lock them up for ever so they can't kill? What happened to 'innocent till proven guilty'?

- **Coca-Cola or Pepsi?** How do *YOU* decide? The

people who sell those brands would love to know. So, researchers looked inside volunteers' brains to see what goes on when they make that choice.[51] And in the UK another study looked at volunteers' brains while they chose between types of baked beans in a supermarket.[52]

If they know how your brain works when it's choosing, it's only another step for them to want to control that choice. Even if they aren't physically changing your brain, a company will want to change the way you think, to make you buy their product. Of course, this is what advertising does – it's the whole point – but do you really want them to know everything that's in your head?

Actually, you can do your bit to fight back. For example, I read that research showed that 75 per cent of shoppers head to the right as soon as they enter a shop, so shops put the expensive things they really want you to buy on the right. So, what do I do? Head stubbornly to the left, with a slight smile on my face, straight to the cheap stuff.

They'll have to try harder than that!

Mind you, what if they installed a secret scanning machine in the doorframe, which would change my thought patterns, and turn me from my normal bolshy, annoying self into a docile and easily led sheep?

All I can tell you is that they haven't done it yet. I'm still turning left.

Messing around with genes

Genes are the tiny building blocks that make us who we are. We inherit some from our fathers and some from our mothers. We have many thousands of them – at the moment, scientists think humans have 20–25,000. And they are very complicated. There are genes for blue eyes, cleverness, height, and hating sprouts; genes for abilities and illnesses. Not all the genes you have will be 'activated'. So, you could have the gene for an illness but not get the illness. Many things involve several different genes all working together. Also, genes can be damaged.

Supposing scientists discovered a gene responsible for fear. Supposing they could get rid of it. Suppose no more – they've done it. In 2005, scientists working with mice discovered a gene responsible for fear.[53] When they bred mice without this gene, the mice showed less fear.

So what? It's a mouse, and mice could probably do with a helping hand in the fear department. Except that fear is there for a reason: in the mouse's case, fear of cats is extremely useful and healthy. Imagine the fearless mouse marching up to a cat and making the mouse-version of a rude sign. One small pounce and your fearless mouse is a dead mouse.

What has this got to do with us? Well, what if the army could select soldiers who had no fear genes? What if you weren't allowed to have a certain job if you had this fear gene? What if scientists found the genes for other natural emotions and you had to be gene-screened before you had certain jobs? Remember that it's not as simple as having one gene for one thing – you could have that particular fear gene but still be incredibly brave, or not have the gene and still be a scaredy-cat for other reasons. But if a test was able to say you had a greater chance of being a scaredy-cat, you might not get the job.

And some fear is important for humans too. You *SHOULD* be frightened of that pan of boiling water, frightened of a rough sea, frightened of an escaped tiger – if you weren't frightened enough you'd be burnt, or drowned, or eaten by the tiger.

Or supposing there was a gene for being violent. Supposing you had it, and your school or parents knew you had it but actually you were very well in control of yourself. Suppose your school wouldn't accept you because of your gene for violence. Or you couldn't get a job. Suppose you had to be specially watched because of your gene for violence.

Imagine your parents had the chance to select embryos without fear genes. Imagine they had – and took – the chance to select an embryo that had the genes for mathematical brilliance, beauty, gorgeous brown eyes, thick hazel hair, patience, sporting skills, musical genius... Would you have been born? I wouldn't.

And what if we could alter genes slightly to make people different? Too late to say 'what if' – we can do it already. It's called gene therapy – it's in its early stages, but it promises cures for many genetic problems. And many opportunities for perfection, if that's what we decide is right.

Brain implants

At the moment, if part of your brain is damaged by injury, or illness, or a stroke, there is little that doctors can do to repair it. In fact, at the moment there's nothing. Your brain sometimes learns to use a different part, so you get some lost skills back after brain injury. A good example is that if you suffer a stroke on the left side of your brain and lose some language skills, you can recover some of them if your right side can be trained to take over the language job.

But what doctors would really like to do is to encourage your brain to repair itself. Or to find a way to insert something into your damaged brain to take over and become part of your brain. You can have an artificial part put in your heart, and doctors would like to do the same with the brain.

It would be wonderful – many people who are currently paralysed could move again, some of those who are deaf or blind could hear and see, patients who have lost their memories could learn to learn again. The possibilities are huge.

And, of course, scientists are working on it. Here are just a few things going on at the moment:

- Scientists are testing how injecting stem cells into human brains can help cure strokes, Huntingdon's disease and Batten's disease.[54]

- Others are planning to test a brain chip to restore damaged memory in rats.[55] If that is successful, they plan to do the same in humans. Unfortunately, because they can't investigate human brain wiring closely enough in advance, they will use an implant modelled on a monkey brain...

- On page 12 I mentioned that one thing a computer can't do is see. But scientists are working on an implant that would imitate the behaviour of the part of the brain that does 'see': the visual cortex.[56]

- At least one team is using the same idea to make an artificial cortex, which could repair damaged parts of our brains.[57] They are trying to find a way to make the artificial neurons communicate with living ones – if they can do this, they will be able to repair any damage and restore lost abilities.

BRAINY FACT The brain implants that some scientists are working on are about a millimetre square. Inside one millimetre of *real* human brain there are four kilometres of axons – the threads that brain cells use to communicate with each other.[58]

Your future brain

Many of these things will be available in your lifetime. They are, at the moment, not in your hands. Some never will be. But, in all the most important ways, your future brain is in your hands. Don't wait for science to bring you a brilliant brain. Do it for yourself. That's what this book has been about.

Look after your brain. It's your greatest gift and without it you can do nothing. There are many things in your life that you will not be able to control. But there is so much you can do to make your brain as good as it can possibly be.

Don't lose it or abuse it. Know it, use it, feed it, grow it, stretch it. Take control of it.

And enjoy it!

HOW WELL DO YOU KNOW YOUR BRAIN NOW?

Whatever you thought at the beginning of this book, your brain has changed, your knowledge has increased, and you have learned more about your own brain than you ever knew was possible.

I'd like you to do one more thing: this quiz. In a notebook or on a piece of paper, write your name and today's date. Then the title: **Know Your Brain Now.**

Read each statement from **A–J** and choose one of these numbers for each one:

1 = agree a lot
2 = agree a bit
3 = don't agree or disagree
4 = disagree a bit
5 = disagree a lot

Then, on your piece of paper, record your answers. So, for example, if you disagreed a bit with statement **A**, write **A4**.

A I know a lot about how the brain works.

1 2 3 4 5

B I have a good brain and I think I am clever.

1 2 3 4 5

C Most people of my age are cleverer than I am.

1 2 3 4 5

D I believe that I will be successful in life.

1 2 3 4 5

E Some people are good at everything.

1 2 3 4 5

F I know exactly what my skills and weaknesses are.

1 2 3 4 5

G I can't change the way my brain is.

1 2 3 4 5

H People who are the cleverest at school
will be most successful later too.

1 2 3 4 5

I Clever people always do well in tests at school.

1 2 3 4 5

J Everyone would learn better if they sat at a
tidy desk, with quiet music in the background.

1 2 3 4 5

Did that seem familiar? At the very beginning of this book, you did a quiz. It was, in fact, exactly the same quiz. Now, you need to compare your answers.

I think some of your answers will have changed. For example, before, you might have thought you couldn't change the way your brain is, or that some people are good at everything – now you know that neither of those things is true. I hope you also have more knowledge about and confidence in your own abilities.

You really have changed your brain. For the better.

BRAIN BOOSTS

Oxygen boosts

- Stand on your head – this helps flood your brain with oxygen. You may need someone to help you with this and you will need a wall to do it against. **DO** make sure you do it somewhere very safe: not near stairs, furniture, water, anything hot or anything fragile. And not if you have just eaten a large meal... Once you are in position, stay upside down for thirty seconds. Afterwards, stand up slowly.

  Don't spend too long upside down – we weren't designed for it. If we were designed to spend a lot of time upside down, we would have feet on our heads.

- Run upstairs four times.
- Go for a **FAST** walk.
- Deep breathing – stand up, as tall as you can; focus on something in the distance. Take a deep, long breath in through your nose, filling the bottom of your lungs and feeling the air slowly fill all the way to the top; hold it for three or four seconds; breathe slowly out through the mouth, till all the air is out. Do this three times.
- Work those arms – stand up where you have plenty of space around you. Stretch your arms straight out to the sides, reaching as far away as you can; raise your arms until your hands meet;

lower and raise, stretching all the time; do this ten times. Then swing them round to the front, passing each other, so that you are hugging yourself, with your right hand round your left shoulder, and left hand round your right shoulder; swing like this ten times. Finally, do windmills with each arm in turn.

- ✪ Upside down bicycling – lie on your back; raise the bottom half of your body, putting your hands underneath your back, until you are supported by your shoulders and upper back; move your legs as though cycling. Do this, nice and fast, for a minute or so.

- ✪ Fresh air boost – go outside for ten minutes of brisk activity: play with the dog/run round the block/kick a ball around in the garden/bounce a ball/walk to the corner shop/do an errand for your mum or dad.

- ✪ Bounce a ball on a tennis racket and see how many bounces you can do without dropping the ball. If you can't find a tennis racket, bounce a ball against a safe wall. Or throw a ball through a basketball hoop. Anything that needs your eye and hand but not your thinking.

- ✪ Yoga balance – stand with feet shoulder-width apart; focus on something in front of you; slowly bring one foot up behind you, until you can hold it in one hand; stand straight, keeping your body strong, and stay as still as possible for about thirty seconds; when balanced, slowly bend forward, holding one arm in front of you, and stay like this for another thirty seconds. Come back to centre and release your foot. Then do the same for the other foot. Try to breathe slowly and deeply.

Happy brain boosts

- Go and do something completely different for half an hour – anything that doesn't involve reading but does involve doing something: practise a musical instrument, or help with the washing up/laundry/dusting.
- Watch a funny programme or read a funny book.
- Phone a friend and have a chat.
- Make a list of five things you like about yourself.
- Do or say something that will make someone else happy. It will make you happy too.
- Total relaxation – lie down somewhere very comfortable (sitting in a chair is fine, as long as you can fully relax). Starting with your feet, tighten and then release the muscles in each part of your body in turn, all the way up to your face. Spend several minutes trying to relax more and more deeply, feeling your legs and arms get heavier and heavier.
- Use your imagination – while relaxed (as above), imagine a place of total peace, perhaps an empty beach on a hot day, or floating on a lilo in a swimming pool with no one else there. Imagine

every aspect of it – the smells, the sounds, the feelings. Only come away from it when you are ready.

Fuel boosts

If you don't have the right ingredients in the house, could you possibly ask for them? You're in training – you need brain food!

- More than water – get a glass of water and drink it with your eyes closed, thinking about the feeling, taste, and what you feel like inside.
- A banana or other piece of fruit – you can have a piece of chocolate with it if you like!
- A protein-packed sandwich on wholegrain bread – i.e. including cheese, egg, chicken, ham, tuna, spicy bean pâté, peanut butter, hummus.
- Any one of these: hummus, yogurt, handful of nuts/seeds.
- Yogurt sprinkled with, for example, sunflower seeds and a few berries.
- Home-made energy shake – in an electric blender, blend a glass of milk with either:
  1 banana + dessertspoon of wheatgerm;
  2 handful of any berries: e.g. strawberries, blueberries, raspberries + teaspoon of honey + wheatgerm;
  3 banana + two heaped teaspoons unsweetened cocoa powder.
- Home-made oat biscuits, flapjacks, banana bread

or carrot cake.
- ⊗ Brain cake – the recipe you have been waiting for! Here it is:

Brain cake recipe

A healthy snack – lower in sugar than normal cakes, with no artificial ingredients, and packed with dried fruit and nuts for long-lasting brain fuel. Linseeds and other nuts and seeds are an excellent source of omega oils, while cranberries and blueberries are also regarded as 'super foods'. Most importantly, this cake is delicious!

Ingredients

100g butter at room temperature (or unsaturated cooking fat)
75g soft brown sugar (or caster sugar)
2 large eggs (omega-rich if you have them)
200g self-raising flour, sieved
1 teaspoon baking powder
Pinch of salt
2 large/3 small ripe bananas mashed until smooth (overripe ones are perfect)
2 heaped dessertspoons linseeds
Juice and grated zest of 1 lemon (or a few drops of lemon oil if you have it)
1 desertspoon milk or water
Plus 200g total of the following: dried cranberries, dried blueberries, chopped dried apricots, pumpkin

seeds. Or choose any 200g combination of seeds, dried apple/other fruit, raisins, flaked almonds, chopped walnuts/any nuts, chopped very dark chocolate – all nutritious and very good brain energy foods.

What to do

1 Line a 2lb loaf tin and line with baking parchment. Heat the oven to 170°/160°fan/Gas mark 3.

2 Mix the butter, sugar, eggs, flour, baking powder, salt and lemon zest or oil with an electric beater. The mixture should drop from a wooden spoon when lightly tapped against the side of the bowl. If not, add a dessertspoon of milk or water.

3 Gently fold the bananas, linseeds and nuts/seeds/fruit into the mixture with a metal spoon. Do not over-mix.

4 Immediately tip the mixture into the prepared tin. Don't smooth it down.

5 Put in the middle of the oven for 50–60 minutes. Check after 50 minutes. The cake is ready when you can put a knife into it and it comes out clean.

6 Remove from the oven and leave in the tin for 10 minutes. Turn out and cool on a wire rack.

GLOSSARY

acetylcholine essential chemical for sending messages in the brain from choline in the diet

ADHD/ADD condition making it difficult to concentrate, behave or sit still

Alzheimer's disease condition that gradually destroys parts of a person's brain so that they cannot think so well; found in older people

ampakines new type of medicine – may be useful for many learning/sleep/memory problems

amino acids tiny substances that help build proteins; our bodies produce some of them but some only come from the foods we eat

amygdala small part of the limbic system on each side of the brain; important in emotions such as fear, anger and joy

antioxidants nutrients that have well-known health benefits; they seem to protect against harmful particles called 'free radicals' (which can cause cancer, for example). Antioxidants are especially found in berries (especially brightly coloured ones like cranberries, blueberries and strawberries), bright or dark vegetables and dark chocolate

artificial sweeteners low-calorie chemicals used to make food or drink sweet without using sugar

Asperger's a mild form of autism – people can be very intelligent but find relationships and conversation difficult because they are not good at understanding the feelings of other people

auditory to do with hearing

axon long stalk of a neuron (nerve cell); carries messages to the dendrites of other neurons

B vitamins group of vitamins responsible for many aspects of health, including emotion and mood

blood pressure how hard your heart has to pump to push your blood round – lower blood pressure is generally better than higher

brainstem where your brain joins your spinal column/neck – responsible for the most basic functions, such as breathing and heart rate

Broca's area part of the language area (usually on the left side of the brain), especially important for speaking with correct grammar

caffeine found mainly in coffee and tea, as well as dark chocolate – can make you more awake

calcium mineral found in, for example dairy foods and beans – helps build bones and teeth

calories the energy in food that we need to keep our bodies working; you need to consume enough calories (from the right foods) to fuel your body properly but if you consume more than your body uses over a period of time you will put on weight

carbohydrates a group of foods that provide energy

cerebellum part of the brain, underneath the main brain; important for learning and movement

choline important nutrient, helps produce acetylcholine in the brain; found especially in eggs, milk, soya, liver, cauliflower, nuts

clone an exact copy of a creature, without using normal reproduction; instead of using a sperm and egg, scientists use a single cell from elsewhere in the body to make an exact copy with the same genes

corpus callosum thick cable joining the left and right halves of the brain

cortex outer layer of the brain

dendrite part of a neuron, like a branch, sending messages between neurons

dopamine a chemical in the brain, responsible, for example, for excitement, pleasure and alertness

embryo an unborn baby at its very earliest stage – before it becomes a foetus

endorphins chemicals responsible for feeling of wellbeing and removing pain and stress

feng shui Eastern philosophy about how to make your environment right, to increase happiness and decrease stress – believers say it brings good luck

fMRI functional magnetic resonance imaging – scan that shows which parts of the brain are being used during a particular activity

folic acid one of the B vitamins, important for brain function

fortified when vitamins and/or minerals are added to foods such as cereals to make them even more healthy

frontal/prefrontal cortex parts of the cortex at the very front of the brain – the prefrontal cortex is nearest to the front and is important for the things we associate with human thought and ability

gene one of the many instructions inside our cells, making us the way we are

glial cell one of the most common cells in the brain, responsible for cleaning up dead cells and feeding the neurons, for example

hemisphere one half of the brain

hippocampus part of the brain very important for memory and learning

hormone chemical produced in the body; controls many different needs and behaviours: sleep, sex, hunger, competitiveness and mood

hypothalamus part of the limbic system of the brain, responsible for many things that we can't control, such as hunger, body temperature, and sleepiness

interpersonal involving understanding how other people might feel, working with other people, caring about other people, leadership skills

intrapersonal involving understanding how YOU feel and work, being in tune with yourself and caring about yourself

kinaesthetic to do with movement

limbic system area deep in the brain with separate parts; important for emotions, instincts and desires

mirror neuron your mirror neurons practise what you see someone else doing, and then you can more easily perform the action yourself

mnemonic a memory 'trick' or special way of

remembering anything

monounsaturated fats there are many different monounsaturated fats/oils – a small quantity is essential in the diet

multisensory involving several senses at once

neurobics exercising the brain, often by making it do things the opposite way from normal

neurofeedback treatment involving controlling your own brainwaves by watching them on a screen and altering thoughts to make them change

neuron brain cell – you have about 100 billion of them. They pass messages to each other, enabling every action and thought

neurotransmitter chemical that allows messages to pass quickly between neurons

nutrients good things in food and drink that give energy or some other benefit

omega oils nutrients in some oils, which we believe give great benefits for brain and body health

pineal gland small gland in the brain, important in controlling our body clock (ability to know rough time of day) and sleep patterns. Scientists are now learning more about it. It has sometimes been thought to have mysterious powers

plasticity the brain's ability to change and adapt – for example, when a part is damaged, another part can sometimes take over. The brain is more plastic than we used to think

polyunsaturated fats there are many different

polyunsaturated fats/oils – very important in the diet, in small quantities

protein important part of our diet; helps protect, repair and build muscle and other body parts

saturated fats types of fat generally regarded as being the least healthy and recommended as only a very small part of the diet; most often found in fatty meats and full-fat dairy products

side effect something that happens when you take a medicine, but was not what was intended. For example, a side effect of some hayfever medicines is sleepiness

spatial to do with the space that something occupies and its appearance. Someone with good spatial awareness may be good at map-reading and puzzles involving pictures

stem cells cells at a very early stage of life, which have the ability to grow into any type of cell in the body: a stem cell may become a nerve cell, skin cell or muscle cell, for example. Scientists hope to use them to help a damaged body repair itself better

stroke when a blood vessel to the brain either blocks or bursts, and an area of the brain is damaged. Strokes can be small or large, and are more common in older people

synapse the tiny gap where the axon of one neuron meets the dendrite of another, and which messages have to cross

thalamus part of the brain's limbic system; all the

senses except smell go through the thalamus

trans-fats / trans-fatty acids fats that have been processed (hydrogenated) and which experts believe are very bad for us. Some research links them to learning problems

tryptophan an amino acid that we can only get from food

tyrosine an amino acid that our bodies can produce (if we have a diet with the right nutrients), but which we can also get from food

vegan someone who chooses to eat nothing that comes from animals – including eggs and milk

visual to do with sight

Wernicke's area part of the language area of the brain (usually on the left side), especially important for understanding meaning

ENDNOTES

Scientists like to know where information comes from, so that they can read more about it and judge how good the information is. I have listed my main sources here, in case you or your parents or teachers want to find out more. Did you see the little numbers by some words in the book? Each one corresponds to a number on this page. If you use the internet to search for some of the names mentioned in these notes, you'll also find more information yourself.

1 Article in *Brain Behavior and Evolution* Vol. 37, 1991.
2 Dr W H Calvin in his book *The River That Flows Uphill*; article in *Natural History,* 1999–2000.
3 Robin Dunbar explains this in is book *Grooming, Gossip, and the Evolution of Language.*
4 There's loads of amazing info about the amazing teenage brain in my other book *Blame My Brain.*
5 More amazing info about this brain stage in *Blame My Brain.*
6 See *Blame My Brain.*
7 The inferior parietal region, on both sides – according to scientists at McMaster University, in 1999.
8 A particular groove in the inferior parietal region.
9 The Sylvian fissure.
10 Dr Eleanor Maguire of the Wellcome Trust Centre for Neuroimaging at University College London led this; with Dr Uta Frith and others.
11 Dr Roger Sperry won the Nobel Prize in 1981 for this work.

12 Michael Gazzaniga and Joseph LeDoux – the patient was special because both sides of his brain could understand and use language, whereas in most people mainly the left side does; so researchers were able to ask questions of each side separately, and the patient would write the right brain's answers with his left hand, and vice versa.

13 This is not simple because both eyes feed info to both halves of the brain, but if you feed the info very quickly to the right or left edge of vision, it will go only to the opposite side of the brain.

14 Robin Dunbar explains current knowledge in *Grooming, Gossip, and the Evolution of Language.*

15 For example *American Journal of Psychiatry* 2002 and J.M. Fuster 1997, The Prefrontal Cortex.

16 A.L. Duckworth and M.E. Seligman of the University of Pennsylvania, Philadelphia.

17 For example, as reported in *New Scientist* May 2005; research reported at the Society for Neuroscience meeting in San Diego, California in 2004.

18 Carried out by Dr Alex Richardson, senior research fellow in physiology at Mansfield College, University of Oxford and Madeleine Portwood, a special educational psychologist for Durham Local Education Authority.

19 Reported in *New Scientist,* May 2005.

20 Carried out at the University of California.

21 Researched by the United States Department of Agriculture.

22 Many research studies, e.g. at University of Iowa College of Medicine. A study in Massachusetts schools in 1987 found that children participating in a school breakfast programme

had better test scores, less lateness and absence. See the Food Research and Action Centre website for some other examples: **www.frac.org/pdf/breakfastforlearning.PDF**

23 For example, researched by Barbara Stewart and others at University of Ulster.

24 Carried out by Dr Trevor Brocklebank, St James's University Hospital, Leeds.

25 Woodchurch Road Primary, Birkenhead, Wirral, Merseyside.

26 Research published in the *Human Psychopharmacology: Clinical and Experimental* July 2006 showed worse memory and concentration 80 minutes after drinking a sugary drink.

27 Government recommended daily allowance – 50g for a girl, 60g for a boy.

28 For example, Dr Fred Gage of the Salk Institute in La Jolla, California; Dr Richard Smeyne of the St Jude Children's Research Hospital in Memphis; Dr Brian Christie of the University of British Columbia.

29 Research in 1999 by H. van Praag, B.R. Christie, T.J. Sejnowski and F.H. Gage reported in *Proceedings of the National Academy of Science*, USA.

30 Study by Daniel Sessler, University of California, published in the *New England Journal of Medicine*.

31 Reported in *New Scientist,* May 2005.

32 At the University of California in San Francisco, led by Dr Marcos Frank, reported in *Neuron*, 2001.

33 For example, by Roger Ulrich, Texas A&M University 1984, and Dr Terry Hartig, University of California at Irvine; Stephen Kaplan from University of Michigan, 1992; Nancy M. Wells, published in *Environment and Behavior,* November 2000;

California Student Assessment Project, 2005.

34 For example, research for the California Board for Energy Efficiency 1999.

35 An Eastern philosophy that many people find helpful. You can find books about it in the library, or research it on the internet. Many of the ideas are good common sense. Others are more strange, but may well work for you.

36 By the University College London, Dr Emrah Duzel, 2006.

37 Howard Gardner is the leader in this field; he introduced the idea in his books *Frames of Mind* in 1983 and Multiple Intelligences in 1993; many authors have written about this since.

38 Emotional intelligence (EQ) was made famous by Daniel Goleman in 1995, but the theory had been discussed by psychologists such as Howard Gardner in the 1970s and 1980s.

39 Including Howard Gardner.

40 Dr Kawashima of Tohoku University in Japan wrote the Brain Training program for Nintendo.

41 Research led by Torkel Klingberg at the Karolinska Institute in Stockholm, reported in *Journal of the American Academy Child and Adolescent Psychiatry*, Vol. 44, p177.

42 Research led by Dr Frances Rauscher and Dr Gordon Shaw.

43 Research by Dr Agnes Chan, Chinese University of Hong Kong, in 2003, reported in *Neuropsychology.*

44 Reported in *New Scientist,* May 2005.

45 Ampakines were pioneered by Dr Gary Lynch of University of California at Irvine.

46 Studied by Julia Boyle and her colleagues at the Surrey Sleep Research Centre at the University of Surrey, UK.

47 Led by Professor John Stein of University of Oxford.

48 Reported from Copenhagen University Hospital, Denmark, published in the *Journal of the American Medical Association,* February 2007.

49 Research led by Prof Vilayanur Ramachandran.

50 A study at Yale University in 2000.

51 Researched by the Baylor College of Medicine in Houston.

52 By the London School of Economics and Political Science, UK

53 Study led by Gleb Shumyatsky of Rutgers University; reported in *Cell* magazine, November 18 2005.

54 Reported in *Scientific American,* February 2007.

55 At the University of Southern California; reported in *Scientific American* Feb 2007; test planned for spring 2007.

56 Kwabena Boahen, now at Stanford University in California, and colleagues at the University of Pennsylvania in Philadelphia.

57 Led by Kwabena Boahen.

58 *New Scientist,* February 3 2007.

Acknowledgements

As always, I have enjoyed the support and enthusiasm of everyone at wonderful Walker Books. Support and enthusiasm would not have been enough without extraordinary hard work from three people in particular: my exceptional editor, Caroline/Caz Royds, lovely assistant editor Gen/Genevieve Herr, and designer extraordinaire Beth Aves. I apologise if any of them turned grey in the process of meeting the toughest deadline ever. I am very grateful to Deborah Lycett, freelance dietician and member of the paediatric group of the British Dietetic Association, who advised on some nutritional aspects – sometimes I went my own way, and any mistakes are entirely mine.

USEFUL WEBSITES
FOR FURTHER INFORMATION

These are all aimed at young people. However, websites can change, so you should ask an adult to check first.

About the brain and learning

'Neuroscience For Kids'

http://faculty.washington.edu/chudler/neurok.html

'Smartkit' – for parents, teachers and older teenagers

www.smart-kit.com

'Family Nutrition' – for families

www.askdrsears.com/html/4/T040400.asp

'The Brain Zone' – for everyone

www.thethinkingbusiness.co.uk/brainzonemainpage.htm

'Scottish Qualifications Authority' – very useful stuff about
learning styles

www.sqa.org.uk/sqa/

'Learning Styles' – a test for children and teenagers

www.bbc.co.uk/keyskills/extra/module1/1.shtml

'BBC'

www.bbc.co.uk/learning/subjects/schools.shtml

Food and health

'Food Standards Agency'

www.eatwell.gov.uk/healthydiet

'Water is Cool in School' campaign

www.wateriscoolinschool.org.uk

Brain training

Tests and games etc

www.brainmetrix.com

Memory

www.memorise.org

Fun exercises

www.brainconnection.com/teasers

INDEX

Page numbers in **bold** refer to the glossary